PSYCHOLOGY
AND
THE OCCULT

from

The Collected Works of C. G. Jung

VOLUMES 1, 8, and 18

BOLLINGEN SERIES XX

PSYCHOLOGY
AND
THE OCCULT

C. G. JUNG

TRANSLATED BY R. F. C. HULL

BOLLINGEN SERIES

PRINCETON UNIVERSITY PRESS

All the volumes comprising the Collected Works constitute number XX in Bollingen Series, under the editorship of Herbert Read (d. 1968), Michael Fordham, and Gerhard Adler; executive editor, William McGuire.

LIBRARY OF CONGRESS CATALOG CARD NUMBER 75-34810
ISBN 0-691-01791-3
PRINTED IN THE UNITED STATES OF AMERICA
BY PRINCETON UNIVERSITY PRESS, PRINCETON, N.J.

First Princeton/Bollingen Paperback Edition, 1977

Second printing, 1981

TABLE OF CONTENTS

FOREWORD

The occult was in the forefront of Jung's interest from the very beginning of his professional career, and before. At the behest of his chief, the great psychiatrist Eugen Bleuler, Jung wrote his M.D. dissertation on "The Psychology and Pathology of So-Called Occult Phenomena,"[1] published in 1902, and evidently composed after he became an assistant physician at the Burghölzli Hospital in 1900. In psychiatric terms, he described several clinical cases of double consciousness, twilight states, and somnambulism, then presented in detail the case of an adolescent girl medium, whose seances he had witnessed in the mid 1890's. He sought to account clinically for the visions experienced by this young woman, and cites the theory of cryptomnesia, the coming into consciousness of unrecognized memory-images—a reference, obviously, to the unconscious. In Jung's conclusion to the monograph, there is an allusion to what sounds very close to the collective unconscious. "I waded through the occult literature so far as it pertained to this subject [the root idea of the girl's visions], and discovered a wealth of parallels with our gnostic system, dating from different centuries, but scattered about in all kinds of works, most of them quite inaccessible to the patient" (par. 149).

Several years earlier, in 1897, while an undergraduate at Basel University, Jung discussed the occult in a lecture to the Zofingia Society, a student club.[2] Speaking in 1897 on the general subject of psychology, the 22-year-old Jung said that the soul does exist, it is intelligent and immortal, not subject to time and space. He declared the reality of spirits and spiritualism, on the evidence of telekinesis, messages of dying people, hypnotism, clairvoyance, second sight, and prophetic dreams.

[1] In the present selection.
[2] These lectures, in manuscript, have been discovered in the files of the Zofingia Society at Basel University, and their publication (for the first time) is now proposed. I am indebted to Dr. Gerhard Adler for a summary of the main thoughts in the lectures.

vii

In February 1905, Jung gave a lecture at his alma mater, Basel University, "On Spiritualistic Phenomena"—a lengthy discourse in which he surveyed the history and psychology of the subject in America and England as well as on the Continent. He drew upon a broad range of literature—Schopenhauer, Swedenborg, Mesmer, Kant, Kerner, Krafft-Ebing, and the famous English physicist Sir William Crookes, whose observations of levitation had impressed Jung particularly. Jung himself had investigated eight mediums in Zurich; in general, he was unimpressed, diagnosing both hysteria and auto-hypnosis in most instances.[3]

Two and a half years later, in a letter of Nov. 2, 1907,[4] Jung told Freud that because of his services as an occultist he had been elected an honorary fellow of the American Society for Psychical Research—nearly two years before he first visited America. He goes on, "In this capacity I have been dabbling in spookery again. Here too your discoveries are brilliantly confirmed. What do you think about this whole field of research?" Unfortunately, Freud's letter in reply is one of the few that is missing. On April 12, 1909, just after Jung's second visit to Freud in Vienna, he writes of a case he is analyzing in which "first-rate spiritualistic phenomena occur" and another that involves the "evil eye," and goes on to refer glancingly to his "spookery" during his last evening with Freud. This was the episode of the poltergeist knocking in Freud's bookcase, which Freud mentioned skeptically in his answering letter: "My dear son, keep a cool head, for it is better not to understand something than make such great sacrifices to understanding." Jung gave a full account only fifty years later in *Memories, Dreams, Reflections*.[5]

Ernest Jones, in his life of Freud,[6] relates that when Freud and Jung met in Munich on December 26, 1910, they had a long talk about occultism, and Freud "was not surprised to hear that Jung had long been fully convinced of the reality of telepathy and had carried out most convincing experiments himself." In a let-

[3] This lecture, serialized at the time in a Basel newspaper, dropped out of sight. It was first republished in vol. 18 of the Collected Works, and is in the present selection.

[4] *The Freud/Jung Letters*, edited by W. McGuire, translated by Ralph Manheim and R.F.C. Hull (Princeton and London, 1974).

[5] Recorded and edited by Aniela Jaffé (New York, 1963), p. 155.

[6] *The Life and Work of Sigmund Freud*, vol. 3 (New York, 1957), p. 387.

ter of May 8, 1911, Jung writes, "The meeting in Munich is still very much on my mind. Occultism is another field we shall have to conquer—with the aid of the libido theory, it seems to me. At the moment I am looking into astrology, which seems indispensable for a proper understanding of mythology. There are strange and wondrous things in these lands of darkness. Please don't worry about my wanderings in these infinitudes. I shall return laden with rich booty for our knowledge of the human psyche. For a while longer I must intoxicate myself on magic perfumes in order to fathom the secrets that lie hidden in the abysses of the unconscious."

This was the letter to which Freud gave a famous reply (12 May 1911): "I am aware that you are driven by innermost inclination to the study of the occult and I am sure you will return home richly laden. I cannot argue with that, it is always right to go where your impulses lead. You will be accused of mysticism, but the reputation you won with the *Dementia* will hold up for some time against that. Just don't stay in the tropical colonies too long; you must reign at home."

And, a month later, astrology again (12 June 1911): "My evenings are taken up very largely with astrology. I make horoscopic calculations in order to find a clue to the core of psychological truth. Some remarkable things have turned up which will certainly appear incredible to you. . . . I dare say that we shall one day discover in astrology a good deal of knowledge that has been intuitively projected into the heavens. For instance, it appears that the signs of the zodiac are character pictures, in other words libido symbols which depict the typical qualities of the libido at a given moment." Freud's reply (15 June 1911) sounds rather fatigued: "In matters of occultism I have grown humble since the great lesson Ferenczi's experiences gave me.[7] I promise to believe anything that can be made to look reasonable. I shall not do so gladly, that you know. But my hubris has been shattered."

*   *

The present selection includes several further and shorter works of Jung's on the subject of the occult, written between 1919 and

[7] Sandor Ferenczi had also been experimenting with the occult. See Jones, loc. cit.

1957. His foreword to a collection of three of these studies, translated into French, forms an introduction to the volume in hand. There are numerous references to occultism also to be found in Jung's letters.[8]

W. M.

[8] *C. G. Jung: Letters*, edited by Gerhard Adler in collaboration with Aniela Jaffé (Princeton and London, 1973, 1976), general index in vol. 2.

PSYCHOLOGY
AND
THE OCCULT

FOREWORD TO JUNG: "PHÉNOMÈNES OCCULTES"[1]

741   The essays collected together in this little volume were written over a period of thirty years, the first in 1902 and the last in 1932. The reason why I am bringing them out together is that all three are concerned with certain borderline problems of the human psyche, the question of the soul's existence after death. The first essay gives an account of a young somnambulistic girl who claimed to be in communication with the spirits of the departed. The second essay deals with the problem of dissociation and "part-souls" (or splinter-personalities). The third discusses the psychology of the belief in immortality and the possibility of the continued existence of the soul after death.

742   The point of view I have adopted is that of modern empirical psychology and the scientific method. Although these essays deal with subjects which usually fall within the province of philosophy or theology, it would be a mistake to suppose that psychology is concerned with the *metaphysical* nature of the problem of immortality. Psychology cannot establish any metaphysical "truths," nor does it try to. It is concerned solely with the *phenomenology of the psyche*. The idea of immortality is a psychic phenomenon that is disseminated over the whole earth. Every "idea" is, from the psychological point of view, a phenomenon, just as is "philosophy" or "theology." For modern psychology, ideas are *entities*, like animals and plants. The scientific method consists in the description of nature. All mythological ideas are *essentially real*, and far older than any philosophy. Like our knowledge of physical nature, they were originally perceptions and experiences. In so far as such ideas are universal, they are symptoms or characteristics or normal exponents of psychic life, which are *naturally* present and need no proof of their "truth." The only question we can profitably discuss is whether they are universal or not. If they are universal, they belong

---

[1] [Paris, 1939. The book is a trans., by E. Godet and Y. Le Lay, of "On the Psychology and Pathology of So-Called Occult Phenomena" (C.W., vol. 1), "The Soul and Death," and "The Psychological Foundations of Belief in Spirits" (both in C.W., vol. 8). The present trans. of the foreword is from the original German MS.]

to the natural constituents and normal structure of the psyche. And if by any chance they are not encountered in the conscious mind of a given individual, then they are present in the unconscious and the case is an abnormal one. The fewer of these universal ideas are found in consciousness, the more of them there will be in the unconscious, and the greater will be their influence on the conscious mind. This state of things already bears some resemblance to a neurotic disturbance.

743 It is normal to think about immortality, and abnormal not to do so or not to bother about it. If everybody eats salt, then that is the normal thing to do, and it is abnormal not to. But this tells us nothing about the "rightness" of eating salt or of the idea of immortality. That is a question which strictly speaking has nothing to do with psychology. Immortality cannot be proved any more than can the existence of God, either philosophically or empirically. We know that salt is indispensable for our physiological health. We do not eat salt for this reason, however, but because food with salt in it tastes better. We can easily imagine that long before there was any philosophy human beings had instinctively found out what ideas were necessary for the normal functioning of the psyche. Only a rather stupid mind will try to go beyond that, and to venture an opinion on whether immortality does or does not exist. This question cannot be asked for the simple reason that it cannot be discussed. More important, it misses the essential point, which is the functional value of the idea as such.

744 If a person does not "believe" in salt, it is up to the doctor to tell him that salt is necessary for physiological health. Equally, it seems to me that the doctor of the soul should not go along with the fashionable stupidities but should remind his patient what the normal structural elements of the psyche are. For reasons of psychic hygiene, it would be better not to forget these original and universal ideas; and wherever they have disappeared, from neglect or intellectual bigotry, we should reconstruct them as quickly as we can regardless of "philosophical" proofs for or against (which are impossible anyway). In general, the heart seems to have a more reliable memory for what benefits the psyche than does the head, which has a rather unhealthy tendency to lead an "abstract" existence, and easily forgets that its consciousness is snuffed out the moment the heart fails in its duty.

745 Ideas are not just counters used by the calculating mind; they are also golden vessels full of living feeling. "Freedom" is not a

4

mere abstraction, it is also an emotion. Reason becomes unreason when separated from the heart, and a psychic life void of universal ideas sickens from undernourishment. The Buddha said:"These four are the foodstuffs, ye bhikkus, which sustain the creatures that are born, and benefit the creatures that seek rebirth. The first is edible food, coarse or fine; touch is the second; the thinking capacity of the mind is the third; and the fourth is consciousness."[2]

[2] *Samyutta-Nikaya*, 12. 11.

1938

ON THE PSYCHOLOGY AND PATHOLOGY OF
SO-CALLED OCCULT PHENOMENA [1]

[1. INTRODUCTION]

1   In that wide domain of psychopathic inferiority from which science has marked off the clinical pictures of epilepsy, hysteria, and neurasthenia, we find scattered observations on certain rare states of consciousness as to whose meaning the authors are not yet agreed. These observations crop up sporadically in the literature on narcolepsy, lethargy, *automatisme ambulatoire,* periodic amnesia, double consciousness, somnambulism, pathological dreaminess, pathological lying, etc.

2   The above-mentioned states are sometimes attributed to epilepsy, sometimes to hysteria, sometimes to exhaustion of the nervous system—neurasthenia—and sometimes they may even be accorded the dignity of a disease *sui generis.* The patients

[1] [Translated from *Zur Psychologie und Pathologie sogenannter occulter Phänomene* (Leipzig, 1902). It was Professor Jung's inaugural dissertation for his medical degree and was delivered before the Faculty of Medicine, University of Zurich. The 1902 title-page stated that the author was at that time "First Assistant Physician in the Burghölzli Clinic" and that the dissertation was approved on the motion of Professor Eugen Bleuler. The book was dedicated to the author's wife, Emma Rauschenbach Jung (1882-1955). A translation by M. D. Eder was published in *Collected Papers on Analytical Psychology* (London and New York, 1916; 2nd edn., 1917). In the following version, the headings have been somewhat re-ordered and some new headings supplied in brackets in an attempt to clarify the structure of the monograph.—EDITORS.

concerned occasionally go through the whole gamut of diagnoses from epilepsy to hysteria and simulated insanity.

3   It is, in fact, exceedingly difficult, and sometimes impossible, to distinguish these states from the various types of neurosis, but on the other hand certain features point beyond pathological inferiority to something more than a merely analogical relationship with the phenomena of normal psychology, and even with the psychology of the supranormal, that of genius.

4   However varied the individual phenomena may be in themselves, there is certainly no case that cannot be related by means of some intermediate case to others that are typical. This relationship extends deep into the clinical pictures of hysteria and epilepsy. Recently it has even been suggested that there is no definite borderline between epilepsy and hysteria, and that a difference becomes apparent only in extreme cases. Steffens, for example, says: "We are forced to the conclusion that in essence hysteria and epilepsy are not fundamentally different, that the cause of the disease is the same, only it manifests itself in different forms and in different degrees of intensity and duration." [2]

5   The delimitation of hysteria and certain borderline forms of epilepsy from congenital or acquired psychopathic inferiority likewise presents great difficulties. The symptoms overlap at every point, so that violence is done to the facts if they are regarded separately as belonging to this or that particular group. To delimit psychopathic inferiority from the normal is an absolutely impossible task, for the difference is always only "more" or "less." Classification in the field of inferiority itself meets with the same difficulties. At best, one can only single out certain groups which crystallize round a nucleus with specially marked typical features. If we disregard the two large groups of intellectual and emotional inferiority, we are left with those which are coloured pre-eminently by hysterical, epileptic (epileptoid), or neurasthenic symptoms, and which are not characterized by an inferiority either of intellect or of emotion. It is chiefly in this field, insusceptible of any sure classification, that the above-mentioned states are to be found. As is well known, they can appear as partial manifestations of a typical epilepsy or hysteria, or can exist separately as psychopathic inferiorities, in which case the qualification "epileptic" or "hys-

2 "Über drei Fälle von 'Hysteria magna'" (1900), p. 928.

terical" is often due to relatively unimportant subsidiary symptoms. Thus somnambulism is usually classed among the hysterical illnesses because it is sometimes a partial manifestation of severe hysteria, or because it may be accompanied by milder so-called "hysterical" symptoms. Binet says: "Somnambulism is not one particular and unchanging nervous condition; there are many somnambulisms." [3] As a partial manifestation of severe hysteria, somnambulism is not an unknown phenomenon, but as a separate pathological entity, a disease *sui generis,* it must be somewhat rare, to judge by the paucity of German literature on this subject. So-called spontaneous somnambulism based on a slightly hysterical psychopathic inferiority is not very common, and it is worth while to examine such cases more closely, as they sometimes afford us a wealth of interesting observations.

6   CASE OF MISS E., aged 40, single, book-keeper in a large business. No hereditary taint, except that a brother suffered from "nerves" after a family misfortune and illness. Good education, of a cheerful disposition, not able to save money; "always had some big idea in my head." She was very kind-hearted and gentle, did a great deal for her parents, who were living in modest circumstances, and for strangers. Nevertheless she was not happy because she felt she was misunderstood. She had always enjoyed good health till a few years ago, when she said she was treated for dilatation of the stomach and tapeworm. During this illness her hair turned rapidly white. Later she had typhoid. An engagement was terminated by the death of her fiancé from paralysis. She was in a highly nervous state for a year and a half. In the summer of 1897 she went away for a change of air and hydrotherapy. She herself said that for about a year there were moments in her work when her thoughts seemed to stand still, though she did not fall asleep. She made no mistakes in her accounts, however. In the street she often went to the wrong place and then suddenly realized that she was not in the right street. She had no giddiness or fainting-fits. Formerly menstruation occurred regularly every four weeks with no bother; latterly, since she was nervous and overworked, every fourteen days. For a long time she suffered from constant headache. As accountant and book-keeper in a large business she had a very strenuous

3 *Alterations of Personality* (orig. 1892), p. 2, modified.

job, which she did well and conscientiously. In the present year, in addition to the strains of her work, she had all sorts of new worries. Her brother suddenly got divorced, and besides her own work she looked after his housekeeping, nursed him and his child through a serious illness, and so on. To recuperate, she went on September 13 to see a woman friend in southern Germany. Her great joy at seeing her friend again after such a long absence, and their celebration of a party, made the necessary rest impossible. On the 15th, quite contrary to her usual habit, she and her friend drank a bottle of claret. Afterwards they went for a walk in a cemetery, where she began to tear up flowers and scratch at the graves. She remembered absolutely nothing of this afterwards. On the 16th she stayed with her friend without anything of importance happening. On the 17th, her friend brought her to Zurich. An acquaintance came with her to the asylum; on the way she talked quite sensibly but was very tired. Outside the asylum they met three boys whom she described as "three dead people she had dug up." She then wanted to go to the neighbouring cemetery, and only with difficulty would be persuaded to enter the asylum.

7   The patient was small, delicately built, slightly anaemic. Left side of the heart slightly enlarged; no murmurs, but a few double beats; accentuated sounds in the mitral region. The liver dulness extended only to the edge of the upper ribs. Patellar reflexes rather brisk, but otherwise no tendon reflexes. No anaesthesia or analgesia, no paralysis. Rough examination of the field of vision with the hands showed no restriction. Hair of a very pale, yellowish-white colour. On the whole, the patient looked her age. She recounted her history and the events of the last few days quite clearly, but had no recollection of what happened in the cemetery at C. or outside the asylum. During the night of the 17th/18th she spoke to the attendant and said she saw the whole room full of dead people looking like skeletons. She was not at all frightened, but was rather surprised that the attendant did not see them too. Once she ran to the window, but was otherwise quiet. The next morning in bed she still saw skeletons, but not in the afternoon. The following night she woke up at four o'clock and heard the dead children in the adjoining cemetery crying out that they had been buried alive. She wanted to go and dig them up but allowed herself to be

restrained. Next morning at seven o'clock she was still delirious, but could now remember quite well the events in the cemetery at C. and on her way to the asylum. She said that at C. she wanted to dig up the dead children who were calling to her. She had only torn up the flowers in order to clear the graves and be able to open them. While she was in this state, Professor Bleuler explained to her that she would remember everything afterwards, too, when she came to herself again. The patient slept for a few hours in the morning; afterwards she was quite clear-headed and felt fairly well. She did indeed remember the attacks, but maintained a remarkable indifference towards them. The following nights, except on those of September 22 and 25, she again had short attacks of delirium in which she had to deal with the dead, though the attacks differed in detail. Twice she saw dead people in her bed; she did not appear to be frightened of them, but got out of bed so as not to "embarrass" them. Several times she tried to leave the room.

8   After a few nights free from attacks, she had a mild one on September 30, when she called to the dead from the window. During the day her mind was quite clear. On October 3, while fully conscious, as she related afterwards, she saw a whole crowd of skeletons in the drawing-room. Although she doubted the reality of the skeletons she could not convince herself that it was an hallucination. The next night, between twelve and one o'clock—the earlier attacks usually happened about this time—she was plagued by the dead for about ten minutes. She sat up in bed, stared into a corner of the room, and said: "Now they're coming, but they're not all here yet. Come along, the room's big enough, there's room for all. When they're all there I'll come too." Then she lay down, with the words: "Now they're all there," and fell asleep. In the morning she had not the slightest recollection of any of these attacks. Very short attacks occurred again on the nights of October 4, 6, 9, 13, and 15, all between twelve and one o'clock. The last three coincided with the menstrual period. The attendant tried to talk to her several times, showed her the lighted street-lamps and the trees, but she did not react to these overtures. Since then the attacks have stopped altogether. The patient complained about a number of troubles she had had during her stay here. She suffered especially from headaches, and these got worse the morning

after the attacks. She said it was unbearable. Five grains of Sacch. lactis promptly alleviated this. Then she complained of a pain in both forearms, which she described as though it were tendovaginitis. She thought the bulging of the flexed biceps was a swelling and asked to have it massaged. Actually, there was nothing the matter, and when her complaints were ignored the trouble disappeared. She complained loud and long about the thickening of a toe-nail, even after the thickened part had been removed. Sleep was often disturbed. She would not give her consent to be hypnotized against the night attacks. Finally, on account of headache and disturbed sleep, she agreed to hypnotic treatment. She proved a good subject, and at the first sitting fell into a deep sleep with analgesia and amnesia.

9   In November she was again asked whether she could remember the attack of September 19, which it had been suggested she would recall. She had great difficulty recollecting it, and in the end she could only recount the main facts; she had forgotten the details.

10   It remains to be said that the patient was not at all superstitious and in her healthy days had never been particularly interested in the supernatural. All through the treatment, which ended on November 14, she maintained a remarkable indifference both to the illness and its improvement. The following spring she returned as an outpatient for treatment of the headaches, which had slowly come back because of strenuous work during the intervening months. For the rest, her condition left nothing to be desired. It was established that she had no remembrance of the attacks of the previous autumn, not even those of September 19 and earlier. On the other hand, under hypnosis she could still give a good account of the events in the cemetery, outside the asylum, and during the night attacks.

11   The peculiar hallucinations and general appearance of our case are reminiscent of those states which Krafft-Ebing describes as "protracted states of hysterical delirium." He says:

It is in the milder cases of hysteria that such delirious states occur. . . . Protracted hysterical delirium depends upon temporary exhaustion. . . . Emotional disturbances seem to favour its outbreak. It is prone to relapse. . . . Most frequently we find delusions of persecution, with often very violent reactive fear. . . then religious and erotic delusions. Hallucinations of all the senses are not uncommon. The most frequent and most important are delusions of sight, smell, and touch. The visual hallucinations are mostly visions of animals, funerals, fantastic processions swarming with corpses, devils, ghosts, and what not. . . . The auditory delusions are simply noises in the ear (shrieks, crashes, bangs), or actual hallucinations, often with sexual content.[4]

12   The corpse visions of our patient and their appearance during attacks remind us of states occasionally observed in hystero-epilepsy. Here too there are specific visions which, in contrast to protracted delirium, are associated with individual attacks. I will give two examples:

13   A 30-year-old lady with *grande hystérie* had delirious twilight states in which she was tormented by frightful hallucinations. She saw her children being torn away from her, devoured by wild beasts, etc. She had no remembrance of the individual attacks.[5]

14   A girl of 17, also a severe hysteric. In her attacks she always saw the corpse of her dead mother approaching her, as if to draw her to itself. No memory of the attacks.[6]

15   These are cases of severe hysteria where consciousness works at a deep dream level. The nature of the attacks and the stability of the hallucinations alone show a certain affinity to our case, which in this respect has numerous analogies with the corresponding states of hysteria, as for instance with cases where a psychic shock (rape, etc.) occasioned the outbreak of hysterical attacks, or where the traumatic event is re-experienced in stereotyped hallucinatory form. Our case, however, gets its specific character from the identity of consciousness during the different attacks. It is a "second state," with a memory of its own, but separated from the waking state by total amnesia. This distinguishes it from the above-mentioned twilight states and relates it to those found in somnambulism.

16   Charcot[7] divides somnambulism into two basic forms:

   a. Delirium with marked inco-ordination of ideas and actions.

---

[4] *Text-Book of Insanity* (orig. 1879), p. 498, modified.
[5] Richer, *Études cliniques* (1881), p. 483.
[6] Ibid., p. 487; cf. also Erler, "Hysterisches und hystero-epileptisches Irresein" (1879), p. 28, and Cullerre, "Un Cas de somnambulisme hystérique" (1888), p. 356*.
[7] In Guinon, "Documents pour servir à l'histoire des somnambulismes" (1891).

b. Delirium with co-ordinated actions. This comes nearer to the waking state.

17   Our case belongs to the second group. If by somnambulism we understand a state of systematic partial wakefulness,[8] we must when discussing this ailment also consider those isolated attacks of amnesia which are occasionally observed. Except for noctambulism, they are the simplest states of systematic partial wakefulness. The most remarkable in the literature is undoubtedly Naef's case.[8a] It concerns a gentleman of 32 with a bad family history and numerous signs of degeneracy, partly functional, partly organic. As a result of overwork he had, at the early age of 17, a peculiar twilight state with delusions, which lasted a few days and then cleared up with sudden recovery of memory. Later he was subject to frequent attacks of giddiness with palpitations and vomiting, but these attacks were never attended by loss of consciousness. At the end of a feverish illness he suddenly left Australia for Zurich, where he spent some weeks in carefree and merry living, only coming to himself when he read of his sudden disappearance from Australia in the newspapers. He had complete retrograde amnesia for the period of several months that included his journey to Australia, his stay there, and the journey back. A case of periodic amnesia is published by Azam: [9] Albert X., 12½ years old, with hysterical symptoms, had several attacks of amnesia in the course of a few years, during which he forgot how to read, write, count, and even how to speak his own language, for weeks at a stretch. In between times he was normal.

18   A case of *automatisme ambulatoire* on a decidedly hysterical basis, but differing from Naef's case in that the attacks were recurrent, is published by Proust: [10] An educated man, aged 30, exhibited all the symptoms of *grande hystérie*. He was very suggestible, and from time to time, under the stress of emo-

8 "Sleepwalking must be regarded as systematic partial wakefulness, during which a limited but logically consistent complex of ideas enters into consciousness. No opposing ideas present themselves, and at the same time mental activity continues with increased energy within the limited sphere of wakefulness." Loewenfeld, *Hypnotismus* (1901), p. 289.   8a [See Bibliography.—EDITORS.]

9 *Hypnotisme, double conscience* (1887). A similar case in Winslow, *Obscure Diseases of the Brain and Mind* (1863), quoted in *Allg Z f Psych*, XXII (1865), p. 405.

10 *Tribune médicale*, 23rd year (1890).

tional excitement, had attacks of amnesia lasting from two days to several weeks. While in these states he wandered about, visited relatives, smashed various things in their houses, contracted debts, and was even arrested and convicted for picking pockets.

19   There is a similar case of vagrancy in Boeteau: [11] A widow of 22, highly hysterical, became terrified at the prospect of an operation for salpingitis, left the hospital where she had been till then, and fell into a somnambulistic condition, from which she awoke after three days with total amnesia. In those three days she had walked about thirty miles looking for her child.

20   William James [12] describes a case of an "ambulatory sort": the Reverend Ansel Bourne, itinerant preacher, 30 years old, psychopath, had on several occasions attacks of unconsciousness lasting an hour. One day (January 17, 1887) he suddenly disappeared from Greene, Rhode Island, after having lifted $551 from a bank. He was missing for two months, during which time he ran a little grocery store in Norristown, Pennsylvania, under the name of A. J. Brown, carefully attending to all the purchases himself, although he had never done this sort of work before. On March 14 he suddenly awoke and went back home. Complete amnesia for the interval.

21   Mesnet [13] published this case: F., 27 years old, sergeant in the African regiment, sustained an injury of the parietal bone at Bazeilles. Suffered for a year from hemiplegia, which disappeared when the wound healed. During the illness he had somnambulistic attacks with marked restriction of consciousness; all the sense functions were paralysed except for the sense of taste and a little bit of the sense of sight. Movements were co-ordinated, but their performance in overcoming obstacles was severely limited. During attacks the patient had a senseless collecting mania. Through various manipulations his consciousness could be given an hallucinatory content; for instance, if a stick was placed in his hand, the patient would immediately

11 "Automatisme somnambulique avec dédoublement de la personnalité" (1892).
12 The Principles of Psychology (1890) I, p. 391.
13 "De l'automatisme de la mémoire et du souvenir dans la somnambulisme pathologique" (1874), pp. 105–12, cited in Binet, Alterations, pp. 42ff. Cf. also Mesnet, "Somnambulisme spontané dans ses rapports avec l'hystérie" (1892).

feel himself transported to a battle scene, would put himself on guard, see the enemy approaching, etc.

22   Guinon and Sophie Woltke made the following experiments with hysterics: [14] A blue glass was held in front of a female patient during an hysterical attack, and she regularly saw a picture of her mother in the blue sky. A red glass showed her a bleeding wound, a yellow one an orange-seller or a lady in a yellow dress.

23   Mesnet's case recalls the cases of sudden restriction of memory.

24   MacNish [15] tells of a case of this sort: An apparently healthy young woman suddenly fell into an abnormally long sleep, apparently with no prodromal symptoms. On waking she had forgotten the words for and all knowledge of the simplest things. She had to learn how to read, write, and count all over again, at which she made rapid progress. After a second prolonged sleep she awoke as her normal self with no recollection of the intervening state. These states alternated for more than four years, during which time consciousness showed continuity within the two states, but was separated by amnesia from the consciousness of the normal state.

25   These selected cases of various kinds of changes in consciousness each throw some light on our case. Naef's case presents two hysteriform lapses of memory, one of which is characterized by delusional ideas, and the other by its long duration, restriction of consciousness, and the desire to wander. The peculiar, unexpected impulses are particularly clear in Proust and Mesnet. In our case the corresponding features would be the impulsive tearing up of flowers and the digging up of graves. The patient's continuity of consciousness during attacks reminds us of the way consciousness behaved in the MacNish case; hence it may be regarded as a temporary phenomenon of alternating consciousness. The dreamlike hallucinatory content of restricted consciousness in our case does not, however, appear to justify us in assigning it without qualification to this "double consciousness" group. The hallucinations in the second state show a certain creativeness which seems to be due to its auto-sug-

---

14 "De l'influence des excitations des organes des sens sur les hallucinations de la phase passionnelle de l'attaque hystérique" (1891).

15 *The Philosophy of Sleep* (1830), cited in Binet, p. 4.

gestibility. In Mesnet's case we observe the appearance of hallucinatory processes through simple stimulations of touch. The patient's subconscious uses these simple perceptions for the automatic construction of complicated scenes which then take possession of his restricted consciousness. We have to take a somewhat similar view of the hallucinations of our patient; at any rate the outward circumstances in which they arose seem to strengthen this conjecture.

26   The walk in the cemetery induced the vision of the skeletons, and the meeting with the three boys evoked the hallucination of children buried alive, whose voices the patient heard at night. She came to the cemetery in a somnambulistic condition, which on this occasion was particularly intense in consequence of her having taken alcohol. She then performed impulsive actions of which her subconscious, at least, received certain impressions. (The part played here by alcohol should not be underestimated. We know from experience that it not only acts adversely on these conditions, but, like every other narcotic, increases suggestibility.) The impressions received in somnambulism go on working in the subconscious to form independent growths, and finally reach perception as hallucinations. Consequently our case is closely allied to the somnambulistic dream-states that have recently been subjected to penetrating study in England and France.

27   The gaps of memory, apparently lacking content at first, acquire such through incidental auto-suggestions, and this content builds itself up automatically to a certain point. Then, probably under the influence of the improvement now beginning, its further development comes to a standstill and finally it disappears altogether as recovery sets in.

28   Binet and Féré have made numerous experiments with the implanting of suggestions in states of partial sleep. They have shown, for instance, that when a pencil is put into the anaesthetic hand of an hysteric, she will immediately produce long letters in automatic writing whose content is completely foreign to her consciousness. Cutaneous stimuli in anaesthetic regions are sometimes perceived as visual images, or at least as vivid and unexpected visual ideas. These independent transmutations of simple stimuli must be regarded as the primary phenomenon in the formation of somnambulistic dream pictures. In excep-

tional cases, analogous phenomena occur even within the sphere of waking consciousness. Goethe,[16] for instance, says that when he sat down, lowered his head, and vividly conjured up the image of a flower, he saw it undergoing changes of its own accord, as if entering into new combinations of form. In the half-waking state these phenomena occur fairly often as hypnagogic hallucinations. Goethe's automatisms differ from truly somnambulistic ones, because in his case the initial idea is conscious, and the development of the automatism keeps within the bounds laid down by the initial idea, that is to say, within the purely motor or visual area.

29   If the initial idea sinks below the threshold, or if it was never conscious at all and its automatic development encroaches on areas in the immediate vicinity, then it is impossible to differentiate between waking automatisms and those of the somnambulistic state. This happens, for instance, if the perception of a flower associates itself with the idea of a hand plucking the flower, or with the idea of the smell of a flower. The only criterion of distinction is then simply "more" or "less": in one case we speak of "normal waking hallucinations" and in the other of "somnambulistic dream visions." The interpretation of our patient's attacks as hysterical becomes more certain if we can prove that the hallucinations were probably psychogenic in origin. This is further supported by her complaints (headache and tendovaginitis), which proved amenable to treatment by suggestion. The only aspect that the diagnosis of "hysteria" does not take sufficiently into account is the aetiological factor, for we would after all expect a priori that, in the course of an illness which responds so completely to a rest cure, features would now and then be observed which could be interpreted as symptoms of exhaustion. The question then arises whether the early lapses of memory and the later somnambulistic attacks can be regarded as states of exhaustion or as "neurasthenic crises." We

16 "I had the gift, when I closed my eyes and bent my head, of being able to conjure up in my mind's eye the imaginary picture of a flower. This flower did not retain its first shape for a single instant, but unfolded out of itself new flowers with coloured petals and green leaves. They were not natural flowers, but fantastic ones, and were as regular in shape as a sculptor's rosettes. It was impossible to fix the creative images that sprang up, yet they lasted as long as I desired them to last, neither weakening nor increasing in strength." Zur Naturwissenschaft.

know that psychopathic inferiority can give rise to various kinds of epileptoid attacks whose classification under epilepsy or hysteria is at least doubtful. To quote Westphal:

> On the basis of numerous observations I maintain that the so-called epileptoid attacks form one of the commonest and most frequent symptoms in the group of diseases we reckon among the mental diseases and neuropathies, and that the mere appearance of one or more epileptic or epileptoid attacks is not decisive either for the character and form of the disease or for its course and prognosis. . . . As already mentioned, I have used the term "epileptoid" in the widest sense for the attack itself.[17]

30   The epileptoid elements in our case are not far to seek; on the other hand, one can object that the colouring of the whole picture is hysterical in the extreme. As against this we must point out that not every case of somnambulism is *ipso facto* hysterical. Occasionally states occur in typical epilepsy which to experts seem directly parallel with somnambulistic states, or which can be distinguished from hysteria only by the occurrence of genuine convulsions.[18]

31   As Diehl [19] has shown, neurasthenic inferiority may also give rise to "crises" which often confuse the diagnosis. A definite content of ideas can even repeat itself in stereotyped form in each crisis. Mörchen, too, has recently published the case of an epileptoid neurasthenic twilight state.[20]

32   I am indebted to Professor Bleuler for the following case: An educated gentleman of middle age, with no epileptic antecedents, had worn himself out with years of mental overwork. Without any other prodromal symptoms (such as depression, etc.) , he attempted suicide on a holiday: in a peculiar twilight state he suddenly threw himself into the water from a crowded spot on the river bank. He was immediately hauled out and had only a vague memory of the incident.

17 "Agoraphobie" (1872) , p. 158.
18 Pick, "Vom Bewusstsein in Zuständen sogenannter Bewusstlosigkeit" (1884), p. 202; and Pelman, "Über das Verhalten des Gedächtnisses bei den verschiedenen Formen des Irreseins" (1864), p. 78.
19 Neurasthenische Krisen" (1902): "When the patients first describe their crises, they generally give a picture that makes us think of epileptic depression. I have often been deceived in this way."
20 *Über Dämmerzustände* (1901), case 32, p. 75.

33   With these observations in mind, we must certainly allow
neurasthenia a considerable share in the attacks of our patient.
The headaches and the "tendovaginitis" point to a mild degree
of hysteria, normally latent but becoming manifest under the
stress of exhaustion. The genesis of this peculiar illness explains
the above-described relationship to epilepsy, hysteria, and
neurasthenia. To sum up: Miss E. suffers from a psychopathic
inferiority with a tendency to hysteria. Under the influence of
nervous exhaustion she has fits of epileptoid stupor whose interpretation is uncertain at first sight. As a result of an unusually
large dose of alcohol, the attacks develop into definite somnambulism with hallucinations, which attach themselves to fortui-
tous external perceptions in the same way as dreams. When the
nervous exhaustion is cured, the hysteriform symptoms disappear.

34   In the realm of psychopathic inferiority with hysterical colouring, we meet with numerous phenomena which show, as in
this case, symptoms belonging to several different clinical pictures, but which cannot with certainty be assigned to any one
of them. Some of these states are already recognized as disorders
in their own right: e.g., pathological lying, pathological dreaminess, etc. But many of them still await thorough scientific investigation; at present they belong more or less to the domain
of scientific gossip. Persons with habitual hallucinations, and
also those who are inspired, exhibit these states; they draw the
attention of the crowd to themselves, now as poets or artists,
now as saviours, prophets, or founders of new sects.

35   The genesis of the peculiar mentality of these people is for
the most part lost in obscurity, for it is only very rarely that
one of these singular personalities can be subjected to exact
observation. In view of the—sometimes—great historical significance of such persons, it were much to be wished that we had
enough scientific material to give us closer insight into the
psychological development of their peculiarities. Apart from
the now practically useless productions of the pneumatological
school at the beginning of the nineteenth century, there is a
remarkable dearth of competent observations in the German
scientific literature of the subject; indeed, there seems to be
a real aversion to investigation in this field. For the facts so far
gathered we are indebted almost exclusively to the labours of

French and English workers. It therefore seems at least desirable that our literature should be enlarged in this respect. These reflections have prompted me to publish some observations which will perhaps help to broaden our knowledge of the relations between hysterical twilight states and the problems of normal psychology.

[2.] A CASE OF SOMNAMBULISM IN A GIRL WITH POOR INHERITANCE (SPIRITUALISTIC MEDIUM)

36   The following case was under my observation during the years 1899 and 1900. As I was not in medical attendance upon Miss S. W., unfortunately no physical examination for hysterical stigmata could be made. I kept a detailed diary of the séances, which I wrote down after each sitting. The report that follows is a condensed account from these notes. Out of regard for Miss S. W. and her family, a few unimportant data have been altered and various details omitted from her "romances," which for the most part are composed of very intimate material.

[Anamnesis]

37   Miss S. W., 15½ years old, Protestant. The paternal grandfather was very intelligent, a clergyman who frequently had waking hallucinations (mostly visions, often whole dramatic scenes with dialogues, etc.). A brother of her grandfather was feeble-minded, an eccentric who also saw visions. One of his sisters was also a peculiar, odd character. The paternal grandmother, after a feverish illness in her twentieth year—typhoid fever?—had a trance lasting for three days, from which she did not begin to awake until the crown of her head was burnt with a red-hot iron. Later on, when emotionally excited, she had fainting-fits; these were nearly always followed by a brief somnambulism during which she uttered prophecies. The father too was an odd, original personality with bizarre ideas. Two of his brothers were the same. All three had waking hallucinations. (Second sight, premonitions, etc.) A third brother was also eccentric and odd, talented but one-sided. The mother has a congenital psychopathic inferiority often bordering on psychosis. One sister

is an hysteric and a visionary, another sister suffers from "nervous heart-attacks."

38   S. W. is of delicate build, skull somewhat rachitic though not noticeably hydrocephalic, face rather pale, eyes dark, with a peculiar penetrating look. She has had no serious illnesses. At school she passed for average, showed little interest, was inattentive. In general, her behaviour was rather reserved, but this would suddenly give place to the most exuberant joy and exaltation. Of mediocre intelligence, with no special gifts, neither musical nor fond of books, she prefers handwork or just sitting around day-dreaming. Even at school she was often absent-minded, misread in a peculiar way when reading aloud—for instance, instead of the word "Ziege" (goat) she would say "Geiss," and instead of "Treppe" (stair) she would say "Stege"; this happened so often that her brothers and sisters used to laugh at her.[21] Otherwise there were no abnormalities to be noticed about S. W., and especially no serious hysterical symptoms. Her family were all artisans and business people with very limited interests. Books of a mystical nature were never allowed in the family. Her education was deficient; apart from the fact that there were many brothers and sisters, all given a very casual education, the children suffered a great deal from the inconsequent, vulgar, and often brutal treatment they received from their mother. The father, a very preoccupied business man, could not devote much time to his children and died when S. W. was still adolescent. In these distressing circumstances it is no wonder that she felt shut in and unhappy. She was often afraid to go home and preferred to be anywhere rather than there. Hence she was left a great deal with her playmates and grew up without much polish. Her educational level was accordingly pretty low and her interests were correspondingly limited. Her knowledge of literature was likewise very limited. She knew the usual poems of Schiller and Goethe and a few other poets learnt by heart at school, some snatches from a song-book, and fragments of the Psalms. Newspaper and magazine stories probably represented the upper limit in prose. Up to the time of her somnambulism she had never read anything of a more cultured nature.

21 [The alternative terms are Swiss dialect. Cf. par. 73, and also "On Hysterical Misreading," pars. 151ff., in C.W. 1.—Editors.]

[Somnambulistic States]

39   At home and from friends she heard about table-turning and began to take an interest in it. She asked to be allowed to take part in such experiments, and her desire was soon gratified. In July 1899, she did some table-turning several times in the family circle with friends, but as a joke. It was then discovered that she was an excellent medium. Communications of a serious nature arrived and were received amid general astonishment. Their pastoral tone was surprising. The spirit gave himself out to be the grandfather of the medium. As I was acquainted with the family, I was able to take part in these experiments. At the beginning of August 1899, I witnessed the first attacks of somnambulism. Their course was usually as follows: S. W. grew very pale, slowly sank to the ground or into a chair, closed her eyes, became cataleptic, drew several deep breaths, and began to speak. At this stage she was generally quite relaxed, the eyelid reflexes remained normal and so did tactile sensibility. She was sensitive to unexpected touches and easily frightened, especially in the initial stage.

40   She did not react when called by name. In her somnambulistic dialogues she copied in a remarkably clever way her dead relatives and acquaintances, with all their foibles, so that she made a lasting impression even on persons not easily influenced. She could also hit off people whom she knew only from hearsay, doing it so well that none of the spectators could deny her at least considerable talent as an actress. Gradually gestures began to accompany the words, and these finally led up to "attitudes passionnelles" and whole dramatic scenes. She flung herself into postures of prayer and rapture, with staring eyes, and spoke with impassioned and glowing rhetoric. On these occasions she made exclusive use of literary German, which she spoke with perfect ease and assurance, in complete contrast to her usual uncertain and embarrassed manner in the waking state. Her movements were free and of a noble grace, mirroring most beautifully her changing emotions. At this stage her behaviour during the attacks was irregular and extraordinarily varied. Now she would lie for ten minutes to two hours on the sofa or the floor, motionless, with closed eyes; now she assumed a half-sitting

posture and spoke with altered voice and diction; now she was in constant movement, going through every possible pantomimic gesture. The content of her speeches was equally variable and irregular. Sometimes she spoke in the first person, but never for long, and then only to prophesy her next attack; sometimes— and this was the most usual—she spoke of herself in the third person. She then acted some other person, either a dead acquaintance or somebody she had invented, whose part she carried out consistently according to the characteristics she herself conceived. The ecstasy was generally followed by a cataleptic stage with *flexibilitas cerea,* which gradually passed over into the waking state. An almost constant feature was the sudden pallor which gave her face a waxen anaemic hue that was positively frightening. This sometimes occurred right at the beginning of the attack, but often in the second half only. Her pulse was then low but regular and of normal frequency; the breathing gentle, shallow, often barely perceptible. As we have already remarked, S. W. frequently predicted her attacks beforehand; just before the attacks she had strange sensations, became excited, rather anxious, and occasionally expressed thoughts of death, saying that she would probably die in one of these attacks, that her soul only hung on to her body by a very thin thread, so that her body could scarcely go on living. On one occasion after the cataleptic stage, tachypnoea was observed, lasting for two minutes with a respiration of 100 per minute. At first the attacks occurred spontaneously, but later S. W. could induce them by sitting in a dark corner and covering her face with her hands. But often the experiment did not succeed, as she had what she called "good" and "bad" days.

41   The question of amnesia after the attacks is unfortunately very unclear. This much is certain, that after each attack she was perfectly oriented about the specific experiences she had undergone in the "rapture." It is, however, uncertain how much she remembered of the conversations for which she served as a medium, and of changes in her surroundings during the attack. It often looked as if she did have a vague recollection, for often she would ask immediately on waking: "Who was there? Wasn't X or Y there? What did he say?" She also showed that she was superficially aware of the content of the conversations. She often remarked that the spirits told her before waking what

they had said. But frequently this was not the case at all. If at her request someone repeated the trance speeches to her, she was very often indignant about them and would be sad and depressed for hours on end, especially if any unpleasant indiscretions had occurred. She would rail against the spirits and assert that next time she would ask her guide to keep such spirits away from her. Her indignation was not faked, for in the waking state she could barely control herself and her affects, so that any change of mood was immediately reflected in her face. At times she seemed barely, if at all, aware of what went on around her during the attack. She seldom noticed when anyone left the room or came into it. Once she forbade me to enter the room when she was expecting special communications which she wished to keep secret from me. I went in, nevertheless, sat down with the three other sitters, and listened to everything. S. W. had her eyes open and spoke to the others without noticing me. She only noticed me when I began to speak, which gave rise to a veritable storm of indignation. She remembered better, but still only vaguely, the remarks of participants which referred to the trance speeches or directly to herself. I could never discover any definite rapport in this connection.

42   Besides these "big" attacks, which seemed to follow a certain law, S. W. also exhibited a large number of other automatisms. Premonitions, forebodings, unaccountable moods, and rapidly changing fancies were all in the day's work. I never observed simple states of sleep. On the other hand, I soon noticed that in the middle of a lively conversation she would become all confused and go on talking senselessly in a peculiar monotonous way, looking in front of her dreamily with half-closed eyes. These lapses usually lasted only a few minutes. Then she would suddenly go on: "Yes, what did you say?" At first she would not give any information about these lapses, saying evasively that she felt a bit giddy, had a headache, etc. Later she simply said: "They were there again," meaning her spirits. She succumbed to these lapses very much against her will; often she struggled against them: "I don't want to, not now, let them come another time, they seem to think I'm there only for them." The lapses came over her in the street, in shops, in fact anywhere. If they happened in the street, she would lean against a house and wait till the attack was over. During these attacks, whose intensity

varied considerably, she had visions; very often, and especially during attacks when she turned extremely pale, she "wandered," or, as she put it, lost her body and was wafted to distant places where the spirits led her. Distant journeys during ecstasy tired her exceedingly; she was often completely exhausted for hours afterward, and many times complained that the spirits had again drained the strength from her, such exertions were too much, the spirits must get another medium, etc. Once she went hysterically blind for half an hour after the ecstasy. Her gait was unsteady, groping; she had to be led, did not see the light that stood on the table, though the pupils reacted.

43 Visions also came in large numbers even without proper lapses (if we use this word only for higher-grade disturbances of attention). At first they were confined to the onset of sleep. A little while after she had gone to bed the room would suddenly light up, and shining white figures detached themselves from the foggy brightness. They were all wrapped in white veil-like robes, the women had things resembling turbans on their heads and wore girdles. Later (according to her own statement) "the spirits were already there" when she went to bed. Finally she saw the figures in broad daylight, though only blurred and fleetingly if there was no real lapse (then the figures became solid enough to touch). But she always preferred the darkness. According to her account, the visions were generally of a pleasant nature. Gazing at the beautiful figures gave her a feeling of delicious bliss. Terrifying visions of a daemonic character were much rarer. These were entirely confined to night-time or dark rooms. Occasionally she saw black figures in the street at night or in her room; once in the dark hallway she saw a terrible copper-red face which suddenly glared at her from very near and terrified her. I could not find out anything satisfactory about the first occurrence of the visions. She stated that in her fifth or sixth year she once saw her "guide" at night—her grandfather (whom she had never known in life). I could not obtain any objective clues about this early vision from her relatives. Nothing more of the kind is said to have happened until the first séance. Except for the hypnagogic brightness and "seeing sparks" there were never any rudimentary hallucinations; from the beginning the hallucinations were of a systematic nature involving all the sense organs equally. So far as the intellectual

reaction to these phenomena is concerned, what is remarkable is the amazing matter-of-factness with which she regarded them. Her whole development into a somnambulist, her innumerable weird experiences, seemed to her entirely natural. She saw her whole past only in this light. Every in any way striking event from her earlier years stood in a clear and necessary relationship to her present situation. She was happy in the consciousness of having found her true vocation. Naturally she was unshakably convinced of the reality of her visions. I often tried to give her some critical explanation, but she would have none of it, since in her normal state she could not grasp a rational explanation anyway, and in her semi-somnambulistic state she regarded it as senseless in view of the facts staring her in the face. She once said: "I do not know if what the spirits say and teach me is true, nor do I know if they really are the people they call themselves; but that my spirits exist is beyond question. I see them before me, I can touch them. I speak to them about everything I wish as naturally as I'm talking to you. They must be real." She absolutely would not listen to the idea that the manifestations were a kind of illness. Doubts about her health or about the reality of her dream-world distressed her deeply; she felt so hurt by my remarks that she closed up in my presence and for a long time refused to experiment if I was there; hence I took care not to express my doubts and misgivings aloud. On the other hand she enjoyed the undivided respect and admiration of her immediate relatives and acquaintances, who asked her advice about all sorts of things. In time she obtained such an influence over her followers that three of her sisters began to hallucinate too. The hallucinations usually began as night-dreams of a very vivid and dramatic kind which gradually passed over into the waking state—partly hypnagogic, partly hypnopompic. A married sister in particular had extraordinarily vivid dreams that developed logically from night to night and finally appeared in her waking consciousness first as indistinct delusions and then as real hallucinations, but they never reached the plastic clearness of S. W.'s visions. Thus, she once saw in a dream a black daemonic figure at her bedside in vigorous argument with a beautiful white figure who was trying to restrain the black; nevertheless the black figure seized her by the throat and started to choke her; then she awoke. Bending over her she saw a black shadow with human outlines, and near it a cloudy white figure. The vision disappeared only when she lighted the candle. Similar visions were repeated dozens of times. The visions of the other two sisters were similar but less intense.

44   The type of attack we have described, with its wealth of fantastic visions and ideas, had developed in less than a month, reaching a climax which was never to be surpassed. What came later was only an elaboration of all the thoughts and the cycles of visions that had been more or less foreshadowed right at the beginning. In addition to the "big attacks" and the "little lapses," whose content however was materially the same, there was a third category that deserves mention. These were the semi-somnambulistic states. They occurred at the beginning or end of the big attacks, but also independently of them. They developed slowly in the course of the first month. It is not possible to give a more precise date for their appearance. What was especially noticeable in this state was the rigid expression of the face, the shining eyes, and a certain dignity and stateliness of movement. In this condition S. W. was herself, or rather her somnambulist ego. She was fully oriented to the external world but seemed to have one foot in her dream-world. She saw and heard her spirits, saw how they walked round the room among those present, standing now by one person and now by another. She had a clear memory of her visions, of her journeys, and the instructions she received. She spoke quietly, clearly, and firmly, and was always in a serious, almost solemn, mood. Her whole being glowed with deep religious feeling, free from any pietistic flavour, and her speech was in no way influenced by the Biblical jargon of her guide. Her solemn behaviour had something sorrowful and melancholy about it. She was painfully conscious of the great difference between her nocturnal ideal world and the crude reality of day. This state was in sharp contrast to her waking existence; in it there was no trace of that unstable and inharmonious creature, of that brittle nervous temperament which was so characteristic of her usual behaviour. Speaking with her, you had the impression of speaking with a much older person, who through numerous experiences had arrived at a state of calm composure. It was in this state that she achieved her best results, whereas her romances corresponded more closely to her waking interests. The semi-somnambulism usually appeared

spontaneously, as a rule during the table-turning experiments, and it always began by S. W.'s knowing beforehand what the table was going to say. She would then stop table-turning and after a short pause would pass suddenly into an ecstasy. She proved to be very sensitive. She could guess and answer simple questions devised by a member of the circle who was not himself a medium. It was enough to lay a hand on the table, or on her hands, to give her the necessary clues. Direct thought transference could never be established. Beside the obvious broadening of her whole personality the continued existence of her ordinary character was all the more startling. She talked with unconcealed pleasure about all her little childish experiences, the flirtations and love secrets, the naughtiness and rudeness of her companions and playmates. To anyone who did not know her secret she was just a girl of 15½, no different from thousands of other girls. So much the greater was people's astonishment when they came to know her other side. Her relatives could not grasp the change at first; part of it they never understood at all, so that there were often bitter arguments in the family, some of them siding with S. W. and others against her, either with gushing enthusiasm or with contemptuous censure of her "superstition." Thus S. W., during the time that I knew her, led a curiously contradictory life, a real "double life" with two personalities existing side by side or in succession, each continually striving for mastery. I will now give some of the most interesting details of the séances in chronological order.

[Records of Séances]

45   FIRST AND SECOND SITTINGS (August 1899). S. W. at once took control of the "communications." The "psychograph," for which an overturned tumbler was used, the two fingers of the right hand being placed upon it, moved with lightning speed from letter to letter. (Slips of paper, marked with letters and numbers, had been arranged in a circle round the glass.) It was communicated that the medium's grandfather was present and would speak to us. There now followed numerous communications in quick succession, mostly of an edifying religious character, partly in properly formed words and partly with the letters transposed or in reverse order. These latter words and

sentences were often produced so rapidly that one could not follow the meaning and only discovered it afterwards by reversing the letters. Once the messages were interrupted in brusque fashion by a new communication announcing the presence of the writer's grandfather. Someone remarked jokingly: "Evidently the two spirits don't get on very well together." Darkness came on during the experiment. Suddenly S. W. became very agitated, jumped up nervously, fell on her knees, and cried: "There, there, don't you see that light, that star there?" She grew more and more excited, and called for a lamp in terror. She was pale, wept, said she felt queer, did not know what was the matter with her. When a lamp was brought she quieted down. The experiments were suspended.

46   At the next sitting, which took place two days later, also in the evening, similar communications were obtained from S. W.'s grandfather. When darkness fell she suddenly lay back on the sofa, grew pale, closed her eyes to a slit, and lay there motionless. The eyeballs were turned upwards, the eye-lid reflex was present, also tactile sensibility. Respiration gentle, almost imperceptible. Pulse low and feeble. This condition lasted about half an hour, whereupon she suddenly got up with a sigh. The extreme pallor of the face, which had lasted all through the attack, now gave way to her usual rosy colour. She was somewhat confused and embarrassed, said she had seen "all sorts" of things, but would tell nothing. Only after insistent questioning would she admit that in a peculiar waking condition she had seen her grandfather arm-in-arm with my grandfather. Then they suddenly drove past sitting side by side in an open carriage.

47   THIRD SITTING. In this, which took place a few days later, there was a similar attack of more than half an hour's duration. S. W. afterwards told of many white transfigured forms who each gave her a flower of special symbolic significance. Most of them were dead relatives. Concerning the details of their talk she maintained an obstinate silence.

48   FOURTH SITTING. After S. W. had passed into the somnambulistic state she began to make peculiar movements with her lips, emitting at the same time gulping and gurgling noises. Then she whispered something unintelligible very softly. When this had gone on for some minutes she suddenly began speaking in

an altered, deep tone of voice. She spoke of herself in the third person: "She is not here. she has gone away." There now followed several sentences in a religious vein. From their content and language one could see that she was imitating her grandfather, who had been a clergyman. The gist of the talk did not rise above the mental level of the "communications." The tone of voice had something artificial and forced about it, and only became natural when in due course it grew more like the medium's own. (In later sittings the voice only altered for a few moments when a new spirit manifested itself.) Afterwards she had no remembrance of the trance conversation. She gave hints about a sojourn in the other world and spoke of the unimaginable blessedness she felt. It should be noted that during the attack her talk was absolutely spontaneous and not prompted by any suggestions.

49 Immediately after this sitting S. W. became acquainted with Justinus Kerner's book *Die Seherin von Prevorst*.[22] She thereupon began to magnetize herself towards the end of the attacks, partly by means of regular passes, partly by strange circles and figures of eight which she executed symmetrically with both arms at once. She did this, she said, to dispel the severe headaches that came after the attacks. In other August sittings (not detailed here) the grandfather was joined by numerous kindred spirits who did not produce anything very remarkable. Each time a new spirit appeared, the movements of the glass altered in a startling way: it ran along the row of letters, knocking against some of them, but no sense could be made of it. The spelling was very uncertain and arbitrary, and the first sentences were often incomplete or broken up into meaningless jumbles of letters. In most cases fluent writing suddenly began at this point. Sometimes automatic writing was attempted in complete darkness. The movements began with violent jerkings of the whole arm, so that the pencil went right through the paper. The first attempt consisted of numerous strokes and zigzag lines about 8 cm. high. Further attempts first produced illegible words written very large, then the writing gradually grew smaller and more distinct. It was not much different from the

22 ["The Clairvoyante of Prevorst," pub. 1829; trans. as *The Seeress of Prevorst*, 1859.—EDITORS.]

medium's own. The control spirit was once again the grand-father.

50   FIFTH SITTING. Somnambulistic attacks in September 1899. S. W. sat on the sofa, leant back, shut her eyes, breathing lightly and regularly. She gradually became cataleptic. The catalepsy disappeared after about two minutes, whereupon she lay there apparently sleeping quietly, muscles quite relaxed. Suddenly she began talking in a low voice: "No, you take the red, I'll take the white. You can take the green, and you the blue. Are you ready? Let's go." (Pause of several minutes, during which her face assumed a corpse-like pallor. Her hands felt cold and were quite bloodless.) Suddenly she called out in a loud solemn voice: "Albert, Albert, Albert," then in a whisper: "Now you speak," followed by a longer pause during which the pallor of her face reached its highest conceivable intensity. Again in a loud solemn voice: "Albert, Albert, don't you believe your father? I tell you there are many mistakes in N's teaching. Think about it." Pause. The pallor decreased. "He's very frightened, he couldn't speak any more." (These words in her usual conversational tone.) Pause. "He will certainly think about it." She went on speaking in the same conversational tone but in a strange idiom that sounded like French and Italian mixed, recalling now one and now the other. She spoke fluently, rapidly, and with charm. It was possible to make out a few words, but not to memorize them, because the language was so strange. From time to time certain words recurred, like *wena, wenes, wenai, wene,* etc. The absolute naturalness of the performance was amazing. Now and then she paused as if someone were answering her. Suddenly she said, in German: "Oh dear, is it time already?" (In a sad voice.) "Must I go? Goodbye, goodbye!" At these words there passed over her face an indescribable expression of ecstatic happiness. She raised her arms, opened her eyes, till now closed, and looked upwards radiantly. For a moment she remained in this position, then her arms sank down slackly, her face became tired and exhausted. After a short cataleptic stage she woke up with a sigh. "I've slept again, haven't I?" She was told she had been talking in her sleep, whereupon she became wildly annoyed, and her anger increased still more when she learned that she was talking in a foreign language. "But I told the spirits I didn't want to, I can't do it, it tires me too much " (Began to cry.)

"Oh God, must everything, everything come back again like last time, am I to be spared nothing?"

51   The next day at the same time there was another attack. After S. W. had dropped off, Ulrich von Gerbenstein suddenly announced himself. He proved to be an amusing gossip, speaking fluent High German with a North German accent. Asked what S. W. was doing, he explained with much circumlocution that she was far away, and that he was here meanwhile to look after her body, its circulation, respiration, etc. He must take care that no black person got hold of her and harmed her. On insistent questioning he said that S. W. had gone with the others to Japan, to look up a distant relative and stop him from a stupid marriage. He then announced in a whisper the exact moment when the meeting took place. Forbidden to talk for a few minutes, he pointed to S. W.'s sudden pallor, remarking that materialization at such great distances cost a corresponding amount of strength. He then ordered cold compresses to be applied to her head so as to alleviate the severe headache which would come afterwards. With the gradual return of colour to her face, the conversation became more animated. There were all sorts of childish jokes and trivialities, then U. v. G. suddenly said: "I see them coming, but they are still very far off; I see her there like a little star." S. W. pointed to the north. We naturally asked in astonishment why they were not coming from the east, whereupon U. v. G. laughingly replied: "They come the direct way over the North Pole. I must go now, goodbye." Immediately afterwards S. W. awoke with a sigh, in a bad temper, complaining of violent headache. She said she had seen U. v. G. standing by her body; what had he told us? She was furious about the "silly chatter," why couldn't he lay off it for once?

52   SIXTH SITTING. Began in the usual way. Extreme pallor; lay stretched out, scarcely breathing. Suddenly she spoke in a loud solemn voice: "Well then, be frightened; I am. I warn you about N's teaching. Look, in hope there is everything needed for faith. You want to know who I am? God gives where one least expects it. Don't you know me?" Then unintelligible whispering. After a few minutes she woke up.

53   SEVENTH SITTING. S. W. soon fell asleep, stretched out on the sofa. Very pale. Said nothing. sighed deeply from time to time. Opened her eyes, stood up, sat down on the sofa, bent forward,

saying softly: "You have sinned grievously, have fallen far." Bent still further forward as if speaking to someone kneeling in front of her. Stood up, turned to the right, stretched out her hand, and pointed to the spot over which she had been bending: "Will you forgive her?" she asked loudly. "Do not forgive men, but their spirits. Not she, but her human body has sinned." Then she knelt down, remained for about ten minutes in an attitude of prayer. Suddenly she got up, looked to heaven with an ecstatic expression, and then threw herself on her knees again, her face in her hands, whispering incomprehensible words. Remained motionless in this attitude for several minutes. Then she got up, gazed heavenward again with radiant countenance, and lay down on the sofa, waking soon afterwards.

Development of the Somnambulistic Personalities

54   At the beginning of many séances, the glass was allowed to move by itself, and this was always followed by the stereotyped invitation: "You must ask a question." Since several convinced spiritualists were attending the séances, there was of course an immediate demand for all manner of spiritualistic marvels, especially for the "protecting spirits." At these requests the names of well-known dead persons were sometimes produced, and sometimes unknown names such as Berthe de Valours, Elisabeth von Thierfelsenburg, Ulrich von Gerbenstein, etc. The control spirit was almost without exception the medium's grandfather, who once declared that "he loved her more than anyone in this world because he had protected her from childhood up and knew all her thoughts." This personality produced a flood of Biblical maxims, edifying observations, and song-book verses, also verses he had presumably composed himself, like the following:

> Be firm and true in thy believing,
> To faith in God cling ever nigh,
> Thy heavenly comfort never leaving,
> Which having, man can never die.
> Refuge in God is peace for ever
> When earthly cares oppress the mind;
> Who from the heart can pray is never
> Bow'd down by fate howe'er unkind.

55   Numerous other effusions of this sort betrayed by their hackneyed, unctuous content their origin in some tract or other. From the time S. W. began speaking in her ecstasies, lively dialogues developed between members of the circle and the somnambulist personality. The gist of the answers received was essentially the same as the banal and generally edifying verbiage of the psychographic communications. The character of this personality was distinguished by a dry and tedious solemnity, rigorous conventionality, and sanctimonious piety (which does not accord at all with the historical reality). The grandfather was the medium's guide and protector. During the ecstasies he offered all kinds of advice, prophesied later attacks and what would happen when she woke, etc. He ordered cold compresses, gave instructions concerning the way the medium should lie on the couch, arrangements for sittings, and so on. His relationship to the medium was exceedingly tender. In vivid contrast to this heavy-footed dream-personage, there appeared a personality who had cropped up occasionally in the psychographic communications of the first sittings. He soon disclosed himself as the dead brother of a Mr. R., who was then taking part in the séances. This dead brother, Mr. P. R., peppered his living brother with commonplaces about brotherly love, etc. He evaded specific questions in every possible way. At the same time he developed a quite astonishing eloquence toward the ladies of the circle, and in particular paid his attentions to a lady whom he had never known in life. He stated that even when alive he had always raved about her, had often met her in the street without knowing who she was, and was now absolutely delighted to make her acquaintance in this unusual manner. His stale compliments, pert remarks to the men, innocuous childish jokes, etc., took up a large part of the séances. Several members of the circle took exception to the frivolity and banality of this spirit, whereupon he vanished for one or two sittings, but soon reappeared, at first well-behaved, often with Christian phrases on his lips, but before long slipping back into his old form.

56   Besides these two sharply differentiated personalities, others appeared who varied but little from the grandfather type; they were mostly dead relatives of the medium. The general atmosphere of the first two months' séances was accordingly solemn and edifying, disturbed only from time to time by P. R.'s trivial

chatter. A few weeks after the beginning of the séances Mr. R. left our circle, whereupon a remarkable change took place in P. R.'s behaviour. He grew monosyllabic, came less often, and after a few sittings vanished altogether. Later on he reappeared very occasionally, and mostly only when the medium was alone with the lady in question. Then a new personality thrust himself to the forefront; unlike P. R., who always spoke Swiss dialect, this gentleman affected a strong North German accent. In all else he was an exact copy of P. R. His eloquence was astonishing, since S. W. had only a very scanty knowledge of High German, whereas this new personality, who called himself Ulrich von Gerbenstein, spoke an almost faultless German abounding in amiable phrases and charming compliments.[23]

57   Ulrich von Gerbenstein was a gossip, a wag, and an idler, a great admirer of the ladies, frivolous and extremely superficial. During the winter of 1899/1900 he came to dominate the situation more and more, and took over one by one all the abovementioned functions of the grandfather, so that the serious character of the séances visibly deteriorated under his influence. All efforts to counteract it proved unavailing, and finally the séances had to be suspended on this account for longer and longer periods.

58   One feature which all these somnambulist personalities have in common deserves mention. They have at their disposal the whole of the medium's memory, even the unconscious portion of it, they are also *au courant* with the visions she has in the ecstatic state, but they have only the most superficial knowledge of her fantasies during the ecstasy. Of the somnambulistic dreams they only know what can occasionally be picked up from members of the circle. On doubtful points they can give no information, or only such as contradicts the medium's own explanations. The stereotyped answer to all questions of this kind is "Ask Ivenes, Ivenes knows." [24] From the examples we have given of the different ecstasies it is clear that the medium's consciousness is by no means idle during the trance, but develops an extraordinarily rich fantasy activity. In reconstructing her somnambulistic ego we are entirely dependent on her subsequent

23 It should be noted that a frequent guest in S. W.'s house was a gentleman who spoke North German.
24 Ivenes is the mystical name of the medium's somnambulistic ego.

statements, for in the first place the spontaneous utterances of the ego associated with the waking state are few and mostly disjointed, and in the second place many of the ecstasies pass off without pantomime and without speech, so that no conclusions about inner processes can be drawn from external appearances. S. W. is almost totally amnesic in regard to the automatic phenomena during ecstasy, in so far as these fall within the sphere of personalities foreign to her ego. But she usually has a clear memory of all the other phenomena directly connected with her ego, such as talking in a loud voice, glossolalia, etc. In every instance, there is complete amnesia only in the first few moments after the ecstasy. During the first half hour, when a kind of semi-somnambulism with reveries, hallucinations, etc. is still present, the amnesia gradually disappears, and fragmentary memories come up of what has happened, though in a quite irregular and arbitrary fashion.

59   The later séances usually began by our joining hands on the table, whereupon the table immediately started to move. Meanwhile S. W. gradually became somnambulistic, took her hands from the table, lay back on the sofa, and fell into an ecstatic sleep. She sometimes related her experiences to us afterwards, but was very reticent if strangers were present. Even after the first few ecstasies, she hinted that she played a distinguished role among the spirits. Like all the spirits, she had a special name, and hers was Ivenes; her grandfather surrounded her with quite particular care, and in the ecstasy with the flower-vision she learnt special secrets about which she still maintained the deepest silence. During the séances when her spirits spoke she made long journeys, mostly to relatives whom she visited, or she found herself in the Beyond, in "that space between the stars which people think is empty, but which really contains countless spirit worlds." In the semi-somnambulistic state that frequently followed her attacks she once gave a truly poetic description of a landscape in the Beyond, "a wonderful moonlit valley that was destined for generations as yet unborn." She described her somnambulistic ego as a personality almost entirely freed from the body: a small but fully grown black-haired woman, of a markedly Jewish type, clothed in white garments, her head wrapped in a turban. As for herself, she understood and spoke the language of the spirits—for the spirits still speak with one another

from human habit, although they don't really need to because they can see one another's thoughts. She did not always actually talk with them, she just looked at them and knew what they were thinking. She travelled in the company of four or five spirits, dead relatives, and visited her living relatives and acquaintances in order to investigate their life and way of thinking; she also visited all the places that lay on her ghostly beat. After becoming acquainted with Kerner's book, she (like the Clairvoyante) felt it her destiny to instruct and improve the black spirits who are banished to certain regions or who dwell partly beneath the earth's surface. This activity caused her a good deal of trouble and pain; both during and after the ecstasies she complained of suffocating feelings, violent headaches, etc. But every fortnight, on Wednesdays, she was allowed to spend the whole night in the gardens of the Beyond in the company of the blessed spirits. There she received instruction concerning the forces that govern the world and the endlessly complicated relationships between human beings, and also concerning the laws of reincarnation, the star-dwellers, etc. Unfortunately she expatiated only on the system of world-forces and reincarnation, and merely let fall an occasional remark concerning the other subjects. For instance, she once returned from a railway journey in an extremely agitated state. We thought at first that something unpleasant must have happened to her; but finally she pulled herself together and explained that "a star-dweller had sat opposite her in the train." From the description she gave of this being I recognized an elderly merchant I happened to know, who had a rather unsympathetic face. Apropos of this event, she told us all the peculiarities of the star-dwellers: they have no godlike souls, as men have, they pursue no science, no philosophy, but in the technical arts they are far more advanced than we are. Thus, flying machines have long been in existence on Mars; the whole of Mars is covered with canals, the canals are artificial lakes and are used for irrigation. The canals are all flat ditches, the water in them is very shallow. The excavating of the canals caused the Martians no particular trouble, as the soil there is lighter than on earth. There are no bridges over the canals, but that does not prevent communication because everybody travels by flying machine. There are no wars on the stars, because no differences of opinion exist. The star-dwellers do not have a human shape but the most laughable ones imaginable, such as no one could possibly conceive. Human spirits who get permission to travel in the Beyond are not allowed to set foot on the stars. Similarly, travelling star-dwellers may not touch down on earth but must remain at a distance of some 75 feet above its surface. Should they infringe this law, they remain in the power of the earth and must take on human bodies, from which they are freed only after their natural death. As human beings they are cold, hard-hearted, and cruel. S. W. can recognize them by their peculiar expression, which lacks the "spiritual," and by their hairless, eyebrowless, sharply cut faces. Napoleon I was a typical star-dweller.

60   On her journeys she did not see the places through which she hastened. She had the feeling of floating, and the spirits told her when she was in the right spot. Then, as a rule, she saw only the face and upper part of the person before whom she wished to appear or whom she wanted to see. She could seldom say in what kind of surroundings she saw this person. Occasionally she saw me, but only my head without any background. She was much occupied with the enchanting of spirits, and for this purpose wrote oracular sayings in a foreign tongue on slips of paper which she concealed in all sorts of queer places. Especially displeasing to her was the presence in my house of an Italian murderer, whom she called Conventi. She tried several times to cast a spell on him, and without my knowledge concealed several slips of paper about the place, which were later found by accident. One of them had the following message written on it (in red pencil):

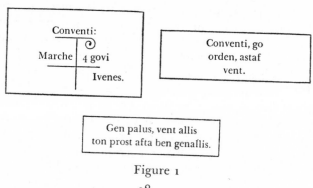

Figure 1

61   Unfortunately I never managed to get a translation, for in this matter S. W. was quite unapproachable.

62   Occasionally the somnambulistic Ivenes spoke directly to the public. She did so in dignified language that sounded slightly precocious, but Ivenes was not boringly unctuous or irrepressibly silly like her two guides; she is a serious, mature person, devout and right-minded, full of womanly tenderness and very modest, who always submits to the opinion of others. There is something soulful and elegiac about her, an air of melancholy resignation; she longs to get out of this world, she returns unwillingly to reality, she bemoans her hard lot, her odious family circumstances. With all this she is something of a great lady; she orders her spirits about, despises von Gerbenstein's stupid "chatter," comforts others, succours those in distress, warns and protects them from dangers to body and soul. She is the channel for the entire intellectual output of all the manifestations, though she herself ascribes this to instruction by the spirits. It is Ivenes who directly controls S. W.'s semi-somnambulistic state.

The Romances

63   The peculiar ghostlike look in S. W.'s eyes during her semi-somnambulism prompted some members of the circle to compare her to the Clairvoyante of Prevorst. The suggestion was not without consequences. S. W. gave hints of earlier existences she had already lived through, and after a few weeks she suddenly disclosed a whole system of reincarnations, although she had never mentioned anything of the sort before. Ivenes, she said, was a spiritual being who had certain advantages over the spirits of other human beings. Every human spirit must embody itself in the course of the centuries. But Ivenes had to embody herself at least once every two hundred years; apart from her, only two human beings shared this fate, namely Swedenborg and Miss Florence Cook (Crookes's [24a] famous medium). S. W. called these two personages her brother and sister. She gave no information about their previous existences. At the beginning of the nineteenth century, Ivenes had been Frau Hauffe, the Clairvoyante of Prevorst, and at the end of the eighteenth cen-

24a [Sir William Crookes, the physicist and psychic investigator.—EDITORS.]

tury a clergyman's wife in central Germany (locality unspecified), in which capacity she had been seduced by Goethe and had borne him a son. In the fifteenth century she had been a Saxon countess, with the poetic name of Thierfelsenburg. Ulrich von Gerbenstein was a relative from that time. The lapse of three hundred years before her next incarnation, and the slip-up with Goethe, had to be atoned for by the sorrows of the Clairvoyante. In the thirteenth century, she had been a noblewoman with the name of de Valours, in the south of France, and had been burnt as a witch. From the thirteenth century back to the time of the Christian persecutions under Nero there had been numerous reincarnations, of which S. W. gave no account. During the Christian persecutions she had played a martyr's part. Then came another great darkness, back to the time of David, when Ivenes had been an ordinary Jewess. After her death as such, she had received from Astaf, an angel in one of the higher heavens, the mandate for her wonderful career. In all her preexistences she had been a medium and an intermediary between this world and the Beyond. Her brothers and sisters were equally old and had the same profession. In each of her preexistences she had invariably been married, and in this way founded a colossal family tree, with whose endlessly complicated relationships she was occupied in many of her ecstasies. Thus, some time in the eighth century she had been the mother of her earthly father and, what is more, of her grandfather and mine. Hence the remarkable friendship between these two old gentlemen, otherwise strangers. As Mme. de Valours she had been my mother. When she had been burnt as a witch I had taken it very much to heart; I had retired to a monastery in Rouen, wore a grey habit, became prior, wrote a work on botany, and died at over eighty years of age. In the refectory of the monastery there had hung a portrait of Mme. de Valours, in which she was depicted in a half-sitting, half-reclining position. (S. W. in the semi-somnambulistic state often assumed this position on the sofa. It corresponds exactly to that of Mme. Récamier in David's well-known painting.) A gentleman who often took part in the séances and bore a distant resemblance to me was also one of her sons from that time. Around this core of relationships there now grouped themselves, at a greater or lesser distance, all the persons in any way related or known to her. One came from the fifteenth century, another was a cousin from the eighteenth century, and so on.

64   From the three great family stocks there sprang the greater part of the races of Europe. She and her brothers and sisters were descended from Adam, who arose by materialization; the other races then in existence, from among whom Cain took his wife, were descended from monkeys. From these interrelated groups S. W. produced a vast amount of family gossip, a spate of romantic stories, piquant adventures, etc. The special target of her romances was a lady acquaintance of mine, who for some undiscoverable reason was peculiarly antipathetic to her. She declared that this lady was the incarnation of a celebrated Parisian poisoner who had achieved great notoriety in the eighteenth century. This lady, she maintained, still continued her dangerous work, but in a much more ingenious and refined fashion than before. Through the inspiration of the wicked spirits who accompanied her, she had discovered a fluid which when merely exposed to the air attracted any tubercle bacilli flying about and formed a splendid culture medium for them. By means of this fluid, which she was in the habit of mixing with food, she had caused the death of her husband (who had indeed died from tuberculosis), also of one of her lovers and of her own brother, so as to get his inheritance. Her eldest son was an illegitimate child by her lover. During her widowhood she had secretly borne an illegitimate child to another lover, and had finally had illicit relations with her own brother, whom she later poisoned. In this way S. W. wove innumerable stories in which she believed implicitly. The characters in these romances also appeared in her visions, as for instance this lady in the above-mentioned vision with its pantomime of confession and forgiveness of sin. Anything at all interesting that happened in her surroundings was drawn into this system of romances and given a place in the family relationships with a more or less clear account of the pre-existences and influencing spirits. So it fared with all persons who made S. W.'s acquaintance: they were rated as a second or a first incarnation according to whether they had a well-marked or an indistinct character. In most cases they were also designated as relatives and always in the same quite definite way. Only afterwards, often

several weeks later, a new and complicated romance would suddenly make its appearance after an ecstasy, explaining the striking relationship by means of pre-existences or illegitimate liaisons. Persons sympathetic to S. W. were usually very close relatives. These family romances (with the exception of the one described above) were all composed very carefully, so that it was absolutely impossible to check up on them. They were delivered with the most amazing aplomb and often surprised us by the extremely clever use of details which S. W. must have heard or picked up from somewhere. Most of the romances had a pretty gruesome character: murder by poison and dagger, seduction and banishment, forgery of wills, and so forth played a prominent role.

Mystic Science

65   S. W. was subjected to numerous suggestions in regard to scientific questions. Generally, towards the end of the séances, various subjects of a scientific or spiritualistic nature were discussed and debated. S. W. never took part in the conversation, but sat dreamily in a corner in a semi-somnambulistic condition. She listened now to one thing and now to another, catching it in a half dream, but she could never give a coherent account of anything if one asked her about it, and she only half understood the explanations. In the course of the winter, various hints began to emerge in the séances: "The spirits brought her strange revelations about the world forces and the Beyond, but she could not say anything just now." Once she tried to give a description, but only said "on one side was the light, on the other side the power of attraction." Finally, in March 1900, after nothing more had been heard of these things for some time, she suddenly announced with a joyful face that she had now received everything from the spirits. She drew forth a long narrow strip of paper on which numerous names were written. Despite my request she would not let it out of her hands, but told me to draw a diagram [fig. 2].

66   I can remember clearly that in the winter of 1899/1900 we spoke several times in S. W.'s presence of attractive and repulsive forces in connection with Kant's *Natural History and*

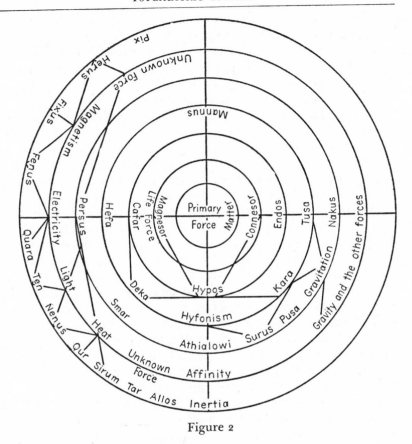

Figure 2

Theory of the Heavens,[25] also of the law of the conservation of energy, of the different forms of energy, and of whether the force of gravity is also a form of motion. From the content of these talks S. W. had evidently derived the foundations of her mystic system. She gave the following explanations: The forces are arranged in seven circles. Outside these there are three more, containing unknown forces midway between force and matter. Matter is found in seven outer circles surrounding the ten inner ones.[26] In the centre stands the Primary Force; this is

25 [Cf. *Kant's Cosmogony* as in His "*Essay on the Retardation of the Rotation of the Earth*" and His "*Natural History and Theory of the Heavens*," ed. and trans. W. Hastie (Glasgow, 1900).—EDITORS.]

26 [Note that the diagram shows only the first seven inner circles.—EDITORS.]

the original cause of creation and is a spiritual force. The first circle which surrounds the Primary Force is Matter, which is not a true force and does not arise from the Primary Force. But it combines with the Primary Force and from this combination arise other spiritual forces: on one side the Good or Light Powers [Magnesor], on the other side the Dark Powers [Connesor]. The Magnesor Power contains the most Primary Force, and the Connesor Power the least, since there the dark power of matter is greatest. The further the Primary Force advances outwards the weaker it becomes, but weaker too becomes the power of matter, since its power is greatest where the collision with the Primary Force is most violent, i.e., in the Connesor Power. In every circle there are analogous forces of equal strength working in opposite directions. The system could also be written out in a single line or column, beginning with Primary Force, Magnesor, Cafar, etc., and then—going from left to right on the diagram—up through Tusa and Endos to Connesor; but in that way it would be difficult to see the different degrees of intensity. Every force in an outer circle is composed of the nearest adjacent forces of the inner circle.

67 THE MAGNESOR GROUP. From Magnesor descend in direct line the so-called Powers of Light, which are only slightly influenced by the dark side. Magnesor and Cafar together form the Life Force, which is not uniform but is differently composed in animals and plants. Man's life-force stands between Magnesor and Cafar. Morally good persons and mediums who facilitate communication between good spirits and the earth have most Magnesor. Somewhere about the middle are the life-forces of animals, and in Cafar those of plants. Nothing is known about Hefa, or rather S. W. can give no information. Persus is the basic force that manifests itself in the forces of motion. Its recognizable forms are Heat, Light, Electricity, Magnetism, and two unknown forces, one of which is to be found only in comets. Of the forces in the sixth circle, S. W. could only name North and South Magnetism and Positive and Negative Electricity. Deka is unknown. Smar is of special significance, to be discussed below; it leads over to:

68 THE HYPOS GROUP. Hypos and Hyfonism are powers which dwell only in certain human beings, in those who are able to exert a magnetic influence on others. Athialowi is the sexual

44

instinct. Chemical affinity is directly derived from it. In the seventh circle comes Inertia. Surus and Kara are of unknown significance. Pusa corresponds to Smar in the opposite sense.

69   THE CONNESOR GROUP. Connesor is the counterpole to Magnesor. It is the dark and evil power equal in intensity to the good power of Light. What the good power creates it turns into its opposite. Endos is a basic power in minerals. From Tusa (significance unknown) is derived Gravitation, which in its turn is described as the basic power manifesting itself in the forces of resistance (gravity, capillarity, adhesion, and cohesion). Nakus is the secret power in a rare stone which counteracts the effect of snake poison. The two powers Smar and Pusa have a special significance. According to S. W., Smar develops in the bodies of morally good people at the moment of death. This power enables the soul to ascend to the powers of Light. Pusa works the opposite way, for it is the power that leads the morally bad soul into the state of Connesor on the dark side.

70   With the sixth circle the visible world begins; this appears to be so sharply divided from the Beyond only because of the imperfection of our organs of sense. In reality the transition is a very gradual one, and there are people who live on a higher plane of cosmic knowledge because their perceptions and sensations are finer than those of other human beings. Such "seers" are able to see manifestations of force where ordinary people can see nothing. S. W. sees Magnesor as a shining white or bluish vapour which develops when good spirits are near. Connesor is a black fuming fluid which develops on the appearance of "black" spirits. On the night before the great visions began, the shiny Magnesor vapour spread round her in thick layers, and the good spirits solidified out of it into visible white figures. It was just the same with Connesor. These two forces have their different mediums. S. W. is a Magnesor medium, like the Clairvoyante of Prevorst and Swedenborg. The materialization mediums of the spiritualists are mostly Connesor mediums, since materialization takes place much more easily through Connesor on account of its close connection with the properties of matter. In the summer of 1900, S. W. tried several times to produce a picture of the circles of matter, but she never got beyond vague and incomprehensible hints, and afterwards she spoke of it no more.

Termination of the Disorder

71 The really interesting and significant séances came to an end with the production of the power system. Even before this, the vitality of the ecstasies had been falling off considerably. Ulrich von Gerbenstein came increasingly to the forefront and filled the séances for hours on end with his childish chatter. The visions which S. W. had in the meantime likewise seem to have lost much of their richness and plasticity of form, for afterwards she was only able to report ecstatic feelings in the presence of good spirits and disagreeable ones in that of bad spirits. Nothing new was produced. In the trance conversations, one could observe a trace of uncertainty, as if she were feeling her way and seeking to make an impression on her audience; there was also an increasing staleness of content. In her outward behaviour, too, there was a marked shyness and uncertainty, so that the impression of wilful deception became ever stronger. The writer therefore soon withdrew from the séances. S. W. experimented later in other circles, and six months after the conclusion of my observations was caught cheating *in flagrante*. She wanted to revive the wavering belief in her supernatural powers by genuinely spiritualistic experiments like apport, etc., and for this purpose concealed in her dress small objects which she threw into the air during the dark séances. After that her role was played out. Since then, eighteen months have gone by, during which I have lost sight of her. But I learn from an observer who knew her in the early days that now and again she still has rather peculiar states of short duration, when she is very pale and silent and has a fixed glazed look. I have heard nothing of any more visions. She is also said not to take part any longer in spiritualistic séances. S. W. is now an employee in a large business and is by all accounts an industrious and dutiful person who does her work with zeal and skill to the satisfaction of all concerned. According to the report of trustworthy persons, her character has much improved: she has become on the whole quieter, steadier, and more agreeable. No further abnormalities have come to light.

[3. DISCUSSION OF THE CASE]

72   This case, in spite of its incompleteness, presents a mass of psychological problems whose detailed discussion would far exceed the compass of this paper. We must therefore be content with a mere sketch of the more remarkable phenomena. For the sake of clearer exposition it seems best to discuss the different states under separate heads.

The Waking State

73   Here the patient shows various peculiarities. As we have seen, she was often absent-minded at school, misread in a peculiar way, was moody, changeable, and inconsequent in her behaviour, now quiet, shy, reserved, now uncommonly lively, noisy, and talkative. She cannot be called unintelligent, yet her narrow-mindedness is sometimes as striking as her isolated moments of intelligence. Her memory is good on the whole, but is often very much impaired by marked distractibility. Thus, despite numerous discussions and readings of Kerner's *Seherin von Prevorst,* she still does not know after many weeks whether the author is called Koerner or Kerner, or the name of the Clairvoyante, if directly asked. Nevertheless the name "Kerner" appears correctly written when it occasionally turns up in the automatic communications. In general it may be said that there is something extremely immoderate, unsteady, almost protean, in her character. If we discount the psychological fluctuations of character due to puberty, there still remains a pathological residue which expresses itself in her immoderate reactions and unpredictable, bizarre conduct. One can call this character "déséquilibré" or "unstable." It gets its specific cast from certain features that must be regarded as hysterical: above all her distractibility and her dreamy nature must be viewed in this light. As Janet [27] maintains, the basis of hysterical anaesthesias is disturbance of attention. He was able to show in youthful hysterics "a striking indifference and lack of attention towards everything to do with the sphere of the perceptions." A notable instance of this, and one which beautifully illustrates

27 "L'Anesthésie hystérique" (1892).

47

hysterical distractibility, is misreading. The psychology of this process may be thought of somewhat as follows: While reading aloud, a person's attention slackens and turns towards some other object. Meanwhile the reading continues mechanically, the sense impressions are received as before, but owing to the distraction the excitability of the perceptive centre is reduced, so that the strength of the sense impression is no longer sufficient to fix the attention in such a way as to conduct perception along the verbal-motor route—in other words, to repress all the inflowing associations which immediately ally themselves with any new sense impression. The further psychological mechanism permits of two possible explanations:

(1) The sense impression is received *unconsciously*, i.e., below the threshold of consciousness, owing to the rise of the stimulus threshold in the perceptive centre, and consequently it is not taken up by the conscious attention and conducted along the speech route, but only reaches verbal expression through the mediation of the nearest associations, in this case the dialect expressions for the object.

(2) The sense impression is received *consciously*, but at the moment of entering the speech route it reaches a spot whose excitability is reduced by the distraction. At this point the dialect word is substituted by association for the verbal-motor speech-image and is uttered in place of it. In either case, it is certain that the acoustic distraction fails to correct the error. Which of the two explanations is the right one cannot be determined in our case; probably both approach the truth, for the distractibility appears to be general, affecting more than one of the centres involved in the act of reading aloud.

74   In our case this symptom has a special value, because we have here a quite elementary automatic phenomenon. It can be called hysterical because in this particular case the state of exhaustion and intoxication with its parallel symptoms can be ruled out. Only in exceptional circumstances does a healthy person allow himself to be so gripped by an object that he fails to correct the errors due to inattention, especially those of the kind described. The frequency with which this happens in the patient points to a considerable restriction of the field of consciousness, seeing that she can control only a minimum of the elementary perceptions simultaneously flowing in upon her. If

we wish to define the psychological state of the "psychic shadow side" we might describe it as a sleep- or dream-state according to whether passivity or activity is its dominant feature. A pathological dream-state of rudimentary scope and intensity is certainly present here; its genesis is spontaneous, and dream-states that arise spontaneously and produce automatisms are usually regarded as hysterical. It must be pointed out that instances of misreading were a frequent occurrence in our patient and that for this reason the term "hysterical" is appropriate, because, so far as we know, it is only on the basis of an hysterical constitution that partial sleep- or dream-states occur both frequently and spontaneously.

75   The automatic substitution of some adjacent association has been studied experimentally by Binet [28] in his hysterical subjects. When he pricked the anaesthetic hand of the patient, she did not feel the prick but thought of "points"; when he moved her fingers, she thought of "sticks" or "columns." Again, when the hand, concealed from the patient's sight by a screen, wrote "Salpêtrière," she saw before her the word "Salpêtrière" in white writing on a black ground. This recalls the experiments of Guinon and Sophie Woltke previously referred to.

76   We thus find in our patient, at a time when there was nothing to suggest the later phenomena, rudimentary automatisms, fragments of dreaming, which harbour in themselves the possibility that some day more than one association will slip in between the distractibility of her perceptions and consciousness. The misreading also reveals a certain autonomy of the psychic elements; even with a relatively low degree of distractibility, not in any other way striking or suspicious, they develop a noticeable if slight productivity which approximates to that of the physiological dream. The misreading can therefore be regarded as a prodromal symptom of subsequent events, especially as its psychology is the prototype of the mechanism of somnambulistic dreams, which are in fact nothing but a multiplication and infinite variation of the elementary process we have described above. At the time of my observations I was never able to demonstrate any other rudimentary automatisms of this kind; it seems as if the originally low-grade states of distractibility gradually grew beneath the surface of consciousness into those

28 *Alterations of Personality,* pp. 205f.

remarkable somnambulistic attacks and therefore disappeared from the waking state. So far as the development of the patient's character is concerned, except for a slight increase in maturity no striking change could be noted in the course of observations lasting nearly two years. On the other hand, it is worth mentioning that in the two years since the subsidence (complete cessation?) of the somnambulistic attacks a considerable change of character has taken place. We shall have occasion later on to speak of the significance of this observation.

Semi-Somnambulism

77   In our account of S. W.'s case, the following condition was indicated by the term "semi-somnambulism": For some time before and after the actual somnambulistic attack the patient found herself in a state whose most salient feature can best be described as "preoccupation." She lent only half an ear to the conversation around her, answered absent-mindedly, frequently lost herself in all manner of hallucinations; her face was solemn, her look ecstatic, visionary, ardent. Closer observation revealed a far-reaching alteration of her entire character. She was now grave, dignified; when she spoke, the theme was always an extremely serious one. In this state she could talk so seriously, so forcefully and convincingly, that one almost had to ask oneself: Is this really a girl of 15½? One had the impression that a mature woman was being acted with considerable dramatic talent. The reason for this seriousness, this solemnity of behaviour, was given in the patient's explanation that at these times she stood on the frontier of this world and the next, and associated just as really with the spirits of the dead as with the living. And indeed her conversation was about equally divided between answers to objectively real questions and hallucinatory ones. I call this state semi-somnambulistic because it coincides with Richet's own definition:

Such a person's consciousness appears to persist in its integrity, while all the time highly complex operations are taking place outside consciousness, without the voluntary and conscious ego seeming to be aware of any modification at all. He will have another person within him, acting, thinking, and willing, without his consciousness, that is, his conscious reflecting ego, having the least idea that such is the case.[29]

78   Binet [30] says of the term "semi-somnambulism":

This term indicates the relations in which this state stands to genuine somnambulism; and further, it gives us to understand that the somnambulistic life which shows itself during the waking state is overcome and suppressed by the normal consciousness as it reasserts itself.

Automatisms

79   Semi-somnambulism is characterized by the continuity of consciousness with that of the waking state and by the appearance of various automatisms which point to the activity of a subconscious independent of the conscious self.

80   Our case shows the following automatic phenomena:

(1) Automatic movements of the table.
(2) Automatic writing.
(3) Hallucinations.

81   (1) AUTOMATIC MOVEMENTS OF THE TABLE. Before the patient came under my observation she had been influenced by the suggestion of "table-turning," which she first came across as a parlour game. As soon as she entered the circle, communications arrived from members of her family, and she was at once recognized as a medium. I could only ascertain that as soon as her hands were placed on the table the typical movements began. The content of the communications has no further interest for us. But the automatic character of the act itself merits some discussion, for the objection might very well be made that there was some deliberate pushing or pulling on the part of the patient.

82   As we know from the investigations of Chevreul, Gley, Lehmann, and others,[31] unconscious motor phenomena are not only a frequent occurrence among hysterical persons and those pathologically inclined in other ways, but can also be induced fairly easily in normal persons who exhibit no other spontaneous automatisms. I have made many experiments on these lines and can fully confirm this observation. In the great majority of cases

29 Richet, "La Suggestion mentale et le calcul des probabilités" (1884), p. 650.
30 *Alterations*, p. 154.
31 Detailed references in Binet, pp. 222ff.

all that is required is enough patience to put up with an hour or so of quiet waiting. With most subjects motor automatisms will eventually be obtained in more or less high degree if not hindered by counter-suggestions. In a relatively small number of cases the phenomena arise spontaneously, i.e., directly under the influence of verbal suggestion or of some earlier auto-suggestion. In our case the subject was powerfully affected by suggestion. In general, the disposition of the patient is subject to all those laws which also hold good for normal hypnosis. Nevertheless, certain special circumstances must be taken into account which are conditioned by the peculiar nature of the case. It was not a question here of total hypnosis, but of a partial one, limited entirely to the motor area of the arm, like the cerebral anaesthesia produced by magnetic passes for a painful spot in the body. We touch the spot in question, employing verbal suggestion or making use of some existing auto-suggestion, and we use the tactile stimulus which we know acts suggestively to bring about the desired partial hypnosis. In accordance with this procedure refractory subjects can be brought easily enough to an exhibition of automatism. The experimenter intentionally gives the table a slight push, or better, a series of light rhythmical taps. After a while he notices that the oscillations become stronger, that they continue although he has stopped his own intentional movements. The experiment has succeeded, the subject has unsuspectingly taken up the suggestion. Through this procedure far better results are obtained than by verbal suggestion. With very receptive persons and in all those cases where the movement seems to start spontaneously, the intended tremors,[32] which are not of course perceptible to the subject, take over the role of agent provocateur. In this way persons who by themselves would never achieve automatic movements of the coarser type can sometimes assume unconscious control of the table movements, provided that the tremors are strong enough for the medium to understand their mean-

[32] As is well known, the hands and arms during the waking state are never quite still, but are constantly subject to fine tremors. Preyer, Lehmann, and others have shown that these movements are influenced in high degree by the ideas predominating in the mind. For instance, Preyer shows that the outstretched hand will draw small but more or less successful copies of figures that are vividly imagined. These intended tremors can be demonstrated in a very simple way by experiments with the pendulum.

ing. The medium then takes over the slight oscillations and gives them back considerably strengthened, but rarely at exactly the same moment, mostly a few seconds later, and in this way reveals the agent's conscious or unconscious thought. This simple mechanism may give rise to instances of thought-reading which are quite bewildering at first sight. A very simple experiment that works in many cases even with unpractised persons will serve to illustrate this. The experimenter thinks, say, of the number 4 and then waits, his hands quietly resting on the table, until he feels it making the first move to announce the number thought of. He lifts his hands off the table immediately, and the number will be correctly tilted out. It is advisable in this experiment to stand the table on a soft thick carpet. By paying close attention, the experimenter will occasionally notice a movement of the table that can be represented thus:

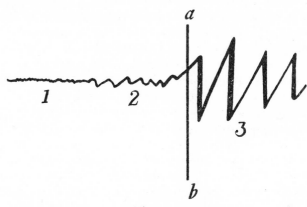

Figure 3

83   *1*: Intended tremors too slight to be perceived by the subject.

2: Very small but perceptible oscillations of the table which show that the subject is responding to them.

3: The big movements ("tilts") of the table, giving the number 4 that was thought of.

ab denotes the moment when the operator's hands are removed.

84   This experiment works excellently with well-disposed but inexperienced persons. After a little practice the phenomenon

usually disappears, since with practice the number can be read and reproduced directly from the intended movements.[33]

85   With a responsive medium these intended tremors work in just the same way as the intentional taps in the experiment cited above: they are received, strengthened, and reproduced, though very gently, almost timidly. Even so, they are perceptible and therefore act suggestively as slight tactile stimuli, and with the increase of partial hypnosis they produce the big automatic movements. This experiment illustrates in the clearest way the gradual increase of auto-suggestion. Along the path of this auto-suggestion all the automatic motor phenomena develop. How the mental content gradually intrudes into the purely motor sphere scarcely needs explaining after the above discussion. No special suggestion is required to evoke the mental phenomena, since, from the standpoint of the experimenter at least, it was a question of verbal representation from the start. After the first random motor expressions are over, unpractised subjects soon begin reproducing verbal products of their own or the intentions of the experimenter. The intrusion of the mental content can be objectively understood as follows:

86   Through the gradual increase of auto-suggestion the motor areas of the arm are isolated from consciousness, that is to say, the perception of slight motor impulses is veiled from the mind.[34] The knowledge received via consciousness of a potential mental content produces a collateral excitation in the speech area as the nearest available means to mental formulation. The intention to formulate necessarily affects the motor component[35] of the verbal representation most of all, thus explaining the unconscious overflow of speech impulses into the motor area,[36] and conversely the gradual penetration of partial hypnosis into the speech area.

[33] Preyer, *Die Erklärung des Gedankenlesens* (1886).

[34] This is analogous to certain hypnotic experiments in the waking state. Cf. Janet's experiment, when by whispered suggestions he got a patient to lie flat on the ground without being aware of it. *L'Automatisme psychologique* (1913), p. 241.

[35] Cf. Charcot's scheme for word-picture composition: (1) auditory image, (2) visual image, (3) motor images, (a) speech image, (b) writing image. In Ballet, *Le Langage intérieur et les diverses formes de l'aphasie* (1886), p. 14.

[36] Bain says: "Thinking is restrained speaking or acting." *The Senses and the Intellect* (1894), p. 358.

87   In numerous experiments with beginners, I have noticed, usually at the start of the mental phenomena, a relatively large number of completely meaningless words, often only senseless jumbles of letters. Later all sorts of absurdities are produced, words or whole sentences with the letters transposed all higgledy-piggledy or arranged in reverse order, like mirror-writing. The appearance of a letter or word brings a new suggestion; involuntarily some kind of association tacks on to it and is then realized. Curiously enough, these are not as a rule conscious associations but quite unexpected ones. This would seem to indicate that a considerable part of the speech area is already hypnotically isolated. The recognition of this automatism again forms a fruitful suggestion, since at this point a feeling of strangeness invariably arises, if it was not already present in the pure motor automatism. The question "Who is doing this?" "Who is speaking?" acts as a suggestion for synthesizing the unconscious personality, which as a rule is not long in coming. Some name or other presents itself, usually one charged with emotion, and the automatic splitting of the personality is accomplished. How haphazard and precarious this synthesis is at first can be seen from the following reports from the literature.

88   Myers gives the following interesting observation of a Mr. A., a member of the Society for Psychical Research, who was experimenting on himself with automatic writing:

89

3RD DAY

What is man? — *Tefi hasl esble lies.*
Is that an anagram? — *Yes.*
How many words does it contain? — *Five.*
What is the first word? — *See.*
What is the second word? — *Eeeee.*
SEE? Shall I interpret it myself? — *Try to!*

90   Mr. A. found this solution: "The life is less able." He was astonished at this intellectual pronouncement, which seemed to him to prove the existence of an intelligence independent of his own. He therefore went on to ask:

Who are you? — *Clelia.*
Are you a woman? — *Yes.*
Have you lived on earth? — *No.*
Will you come to life? — *Yes.*

When? — *In six years.*
Why are you conversing with me? — *E if Clelia el.*

Mr. A. interpreted this answer as: "I Clelia feel."

91
4TH DAY
Am I the one who asks questions? — *Yes.*
Is Clelia there? — *No.*
Who is here then? — *Nobody.*
Does Clelia exist at all? — *No.*
Then with whom was I speaking yesterday? — *With nobody.*[37]

92   Janet conducted the following conversation with the subconscious of Lucie, who, meanwhile, was engaged in conversation with another observer:

[Janet asks:] Do you hear me? [Lucie answers, in automatic writing:] *No.*
But one has to hear in order to answer. — *Absolutely.*
Then how do you do it? — *I don't know.*
There must be someone who hears me. — *Yes.*
Who is it? — *Somebody besides Lucie.*
All right. Somebody else. Shall we give the other person a name? — *No.*
Yes, it will be more convenient. — *All right. Adrienne.*
Well, Adrienne, do you hear me? — *Yes.*[38]

93   One can see from these extracts how the unconscious personality builds itself up: it owes its existence simply to suggestive questions which strike an answering chord in the medium's own disposition. This disposition can be explained by the disaggregation of psychic complexes, and the feeling of strangeness evoked by these automatisms assists the process as soon as conscious attention is directed to the automatic act. Binet remarks on this experiment of Janet's: "Nevertheless it should be carefully noted that if the personality of 'Adrienne' could be created, it was because the suggestion encountered a *psychological possibility*; in other words, disaggregated phenomena were existing there apart from the normal consciousness of the subject." [39] The individualization of the subconscious is always a great step forward and has enormous suggestive

37 Myers, "Automatic writing" (1885).
38 *L'Automatisme,* pp. 317–18.
39 Binet, p. 147.

influence on further development of the automatisms.[40] The formation of unconscious personalities in our case must also be regarded in this light.

94   The objection that the table-turning was "simulated" may well be abandoned when one considers the phenomenon of thought-reading from intended tremors, of which the patient gave ample proof. Rapid, conscious thought-reading requires at the very least an extraordinary amount of practice, and this the patient demonstrably lacked. Whole conversations can be carried on by means of these tremors, as happened in our case. In the same way the suggestibility of the subconscious can be demonstrated objectively if, for instance, the operator concentrates on the thought: "The medium's hand shall no longer move the table or the glass," and at once, contrary to all expectation, and to the liveliest astonishment of the subject, the table is immobilized. Naturally all kinds of other suggestions can be realized too, provided that their innervation does not exceed the area of partial hypnosis (which proves at the same time the partial nature of the hypnosis). Hence suggestions aimed at the legs or the other arm will not work.

95   The table-turning was not an automatism confined exclusively to the patient's semi-somnambulism. On the contrary it occurred in its most pronounced form in the waking state, and in most cases then passed over into semi-somnambulism, whose onset was generally announced by hallucinations, as at the first séance.

96   (2) AUTOMATIC WRITING. Another automatic phenomenon, which from the first corresponds to a higher degree of partial hypnosis, is automatic writing. It is, at least in my experience, much rarer and much more difficult to produce than table-turning. Here again it is a question of a primary suggestion, directed to the conscious mind when sensibility is retained, and to the unconscious when it is extinct. The suggestion, however, is not a simple one, since it already contains an intellectual element: "to write" means "to write something." This special property of the suggestion, going beyond the purely motor sphere, often confuses the subject and gives rise to counter-suggestions which prevent the appearance of automatisms. However, I have noticed

40 'Once baptized, the unconscious personage is more definite and distinct; he shows his psychological characteristics better." Janet, L'Automatisme, p. 318.

in a few cases that the suggestion is realized despite its comparative boldness (it is after all directed to the waking consciousness of a so-called normal person!), but that it does so in a peculiar way, by putting only the purely motor part of the central nervous system under hypnosis, and that the deeper hypnosis is then obtained from the motor phenomenon by auto-suggestion, as in the procedure for table-turning described above. The subject,[41] holding a pencil in his hand, is purposely engaged in conversation to distract his attention from writing. The hand thereupon starts to move, making a number of strokes and zigzag lines at first, or else a simple line.

Figure 4

It sometimes happens that the pencil does not touch the paper at all but writes in the air. These movements must be regarded as purely motor phenomena corresponding to the expression of the motor element in the idea of "writing." They are somewhat rare; usually single letters are written right off, and what was said above of table-turning is true here of their combination into words and sentences. Now and then true mirror-writing is observed. In the majority of cases, and perhaps in all experiments with beginners who are not under some special suggestion, the automatic writing is that of the subject. Occasionally its character may be greatly changed,[42] but this is secondary, and is always a symptom of the synthesis of a subconscious personality. As already stated, the automatic writing of our patient never came to very much. The experiments were carried out in the dark, and in most cases she passed over into semi-somnambulism or ecstasy. So the automatic writing had the same result as the preliminary table-turning.

97   (3) HALLUCINATIONS. The manner of transition to somnam-

[41] Cf. the experiments of Binet and Féré, in Binet, pp. 99ff.
[42] Cf. the tests in Flournoy, *From India to the Planet Mars* (orig. 1900).

bulism in the second séance is of psychological significance. As reported, the automatic phenomena were in full swing when darkness descended. The interesting event in the preceding séance was the brusque interruption of a communication from the grandfather, which became the starting-point for various discussions among members of the circle. These two factors, darkness and a remarkable occurrence, seem to have caused a rapid deepening of hypnosis, which enabled the hallucinations to develop. The psychological mechanism of this process seems to be as follows: The influence of darkness on suggestibility, particularly in regard to the sense organs, is well known.[43] Binet states that it has a special influence on hysterical subjects, producing immediate drowsiness.[44] As may be assumed from the foregoing explanations, the patient was in a state of partial hypnosis, and furthermore a subconscious personality having the closest ties with the speech area had already constituted itself. The automatic expression of this personality was interrupted in the most unexpected way by a new person whose existence no one suspected. Whence came this split? Obviously the patient had entertained the liveliest expectations about this first séance. Any reminiscences she had of me and my family had probably grouped themselves around this feeling of expectation, and they suddenly came to light when the automatic expression was at its climax. The fact that it was my grandfather and no one else—not, for instance, my dead father, who, as the patient knew, was closer to me than my grandfather, whom I had never known—may suggest where the origin of this new person is to be sought. It was probably a dissociation from the already existing personality, and this split-off part seized upon the nearest available material for its expression, namely the associations concerning myself. Whether this offers a parallel to the results of Freud's dream investigations [45] must remain unanswered, for we have no means of judging how far the emotion in question may be considered "repressed." From the brusque intervention of the new personality we may conclude that the patient's imaginings were extremely vivid, with a correspondingly intense expectation which a certain maidenly modesty and embarrassment

43 Cf. Hagen, "Zur Theorie der Hallucination" (1868), p. 10.
44 *Alterations,* pp. 171ff.
45 *The Interpretation of Dreams* (orig. 1900).

sought perhaps to overcome. At any rate this event reminds us vividly of the way dreams suddenly present to consciousness, in more or less transparent symbolism, things one has never admitted to oneself clearly and openly. We do not know when the splitting off of the new personality occurred, whether it had been slowly preparing in the unconscious, or whether it only came about during the séance. In any case it meant a considerable increase in the extent of the unconscious area rendered accessible by hypnosis. At the same time this event, in view of the impression it made on the waking consciousness of the patient, must be regarded as powerfully suggestive, for the perception of the unexpected intervention of a new personality was bound to increase still further the feeling of strangeness aroused by the automatism, and would naturally suggest the thought that an independent spirit was making itself known. From this followed the very understandable association that it might be possible to see this spirit.

98   The situation that ensued at the second séance can be explained by the coincidence of this energizing suggestion with the heightened suggestibility occasioned by the darkness. The hypnosis, and with it the chain of split-off ideas, breaks through into the visual sphere; the expression of the unconscious, hitherto purely motor, is objectified (in accordance with the specific energy of the newly created system) in the form of visual images having the character of an hallucination—not as a mere accompaniment of the verbal automatism but as a direct substitute function. The explanation of the unexpected situation that arose in the first séance, at the time quite inexplicable, is no longer given in words, but as an allegorical vision. The proposition "they do not hate one another, but are friends" is expressed in a picture of the two grandfathers arm-in-arm. We frequently come across such things in somnambulism: the thinking of somnambulists proceeds in plastic images which constantly break through into this or that sensory sphere and are objectified as hallucinations. The thought process sinks into the subconscious and only its final terms reach consciousness directly as hallucinations or as vivid and sensuously coloured ideas. In our case the same thing occurred as with the patient whose anaesthetic hand Binet pricked nine times, making her think vividly of the number 9; or Flournoy's Hélène Smith, who, on

being asked in her shop about a certain pattern, suddenly saw before her the figure 18, eight to ten inches high, representing the number of days the pattern had been on loan.[46] The question arises as to why the automatism broke through in the visual sphere and not in the acoustic. There are several reasons for this choice of the visual:

99   (a) The patient was not gifted acoustically; she was for instance very unmusical.

(b) There was no silence (to correspond with the darkness) which might have favoured the occurrence of auditory hallucinations, for we were talking all the time.

(c) The heightened conviction of the near presence of spirits, owing to the feeling of strangeness evoked by the automatism, could easily lead to the idea that it might be possible to see a spirit, thus causing a slight excitation of the visual sphere.

(d) The entoptic phenomena in the darkness favoured the appearance of hallucinations.

00   The reasons given in (c) and (d) are of decisive importance for the appearance of hallucinations. The entoptic phenomena in this case play the same role in producing automatisms by auto-suggestion as do the slight tactile stimuli during hypnosis of the motor centres. As reported, the patient saw sparks before passing into the first hallucinatory twilight state at the first séance. Obviously attention was already at high pitch and directed to visual perceptions, so that the light sensations of the retina, usually very weak, were seen with great intensity. The part played by entoptic perceptions of light in the production of hallucinations deserves closer scrutiny. Schüle says: "The swarm of lights and colours that excite and activate the nocturnal field of vision in the darkness supplies the material for the fantastic figures seen in the air before going to sleep." [47] As we know, we never see absolute darkness, always a few patches of the dark field are dully illuminated; flecks of light bob up here and there and combine into all sorts of shapes, and it only needs a moderately active imagination to form out of them, as one does out of clouds, certain figures known to oneself personally. As one falls asleep, one's fading power of judgment

46 India to Mars, p. 59.
47 Handbuch der Geisteskrankheiten (1878), p. 134.

leaves the imagination free to construct more and more vivid forms. "Instead of the spots of light, the haziness and changing colours of the dark visual field, outlines of definite objects begin to appear." [48] Hypnagogic hallucinations arise in this way. Naturally the chief share falls to the imagination, which is why highly imaginative people are particularly subject to them.[49] The "hypnopompic" hallucinations described by Myers are essentially the same as the hypnagogic ones.

101   It is very probable that hypnagogic images are identical with the dream-images of normal sleep, or that they form their visual foundation. Maury [50] has proved by self-observation that the images which floated round him hypnagogically were also the objects of the dreams that followed. Ladd [51] showed the same thing even more convincingly. With practice he succeeded in waking himself up two to five minutes after falling asleep. Each time he noticed that the bright figures dancing before the retina formed as it were the outlines of the images just dreamed of. He even supposes that practically all visual dreams derive their formal elements from the light sensations of the retina. In our case the situation favoured the development of a fantastic interpretation. Also, we must not underrate the influence of the tense expectation which caused the dull light sensations of the retina to appear with increased intensity.[52] The development

[48] Müller, *Phantastische Gesichtserscheinungen* (1826), quoted by Hagen in "Zur Theorie der Hallucination" (1868), p. 41.

[49] Spinoza had a hypnopompic vision of a "nigrum et scabiosum Brasilianum" (a dirty black Brazilian)—Hagen, "Zur Theorie der Hallucination" (1868), p. 49. In Goethe's *Elective Affinities,* Ottilie sometimes saw in the half darkness the figure of Eduard in a dimly lit room. Cf. also Jerome Cardan, *De subtilitate rerum:* "Imagines videbam ab imo lecti, quasi e parvulis annulis arcisque constantes, arborum, belluarum, hominum, oppidorum, instructarum acierum, bellicorum et musicorum instrumentorum aliorumque huius generis adscendentes, vicissimque descendentes, aliis atque aliis succedentibus" (At the foot of the bed I saw images, consisting as it were of small circles and curves, and representing trees, animals, men, towns, troops drawn up in line, instruments of war and of music and other like things, rising and falling in turn, and coming one after another).

[50] *Le Sommeil et les rêves* (1861), p. 134.

[51] "Psychology of Visual Dreams" (1892).

[52] Hecker says of these states (*Über Visionen,* 1848, p. 16): "There is a simple, elementary vision caused by mental over-activity, without fantastic imagery, without even sensuous ideas: it is the vision of formless light, a manifestation of the visual organ stimulated from within."

of retinal phenomena then followed in accordance with the predominant ideas. Hallucinations have been observed to arise in this way with other visionaries: Joan of Arc saw first a cloud of light,[53] then out of it, a little later, stepped St. Michael, St. Catharine, and St. Margaret. Swedenborg saw nothing for a whole hour but luminous spheres and brilliant flames.[54] All the time he felt a tremendous change going on in his brain, which seemed to him like a "release of light." An hour afterwards he suddenly saw real figures whom he took to be angels and spirits. The sun vision of Benvenuto Cellini in Sant' Angelo probably belongs to the same category.[55] A student who often saw apparitions said: "When these apparitions come, I see at first only single masses of light and hear at the same time a dull roaring in my ears. But after a bit these outlines turn into distinct figures." [56] The hallucinations arise in quite the classical way with Flournoy's Hélène Smith. I cite the relevant passages from his report:

March 18. Attempt to experiment in the darkness. . . . Mlle. Smith sees a balloon, now luminous, now becoming dark.

March 25. . . . Mlle. Smith begins to distinguish vague gleams with long white streamers moving from the floor to the ceiling, and then a magnificent star, which in the darkness appears to her alone throughout the whole séance.

April 1. Mlle. Smith is very much agitated; she has fits of shivering, is very cold. She is very restless, and sees suddenly, hovering above the table, a grinning, very ugly face, with long red hair. Afterwards she sees a magnificent bouquet of roses of different hues. . . . Suddenly she sees a small snake come out from underneath the bouquet; it rises up gently, smells the flowers, looks at them . . .[57]

Concerning the origin of her Mars visions, Hélène Smith said: "The red light continues about me, and I find myself surrounded by extraordinary flowers. . . ." [58]

At all times the complex hallucinations of visionaries have occupied a special place in scientific criticism. Thus, quite early,

53 Quicherat, *Procès de condamnation et de réhabilitation de Jeanne d'Arc* (1841–49), V, pp. 116f.
54 Hagen (1868), p. 57.
55 *Life of Cellini* (trans. by Symonds), pp. 231f.
56 Hagen (1868), p. 57.
57 Flournoy, *India to Mars*, pp. 36ff. (trans. modified).
58 Ibid., p. 170.

Macario [59] distinguished them as "intuitive" hallucinations from ordinary hallucinations, saying that they occur in persons of lively mind, deep understanding, and high nervous excitability. Hecker expresses himself in a similar manner but even more enthusiastically. He supposes their conditioning factor to be the "congenitally high development of the psychic organ, which through its spontaneous activity calls the life of the imagination into free and nimble play." [60] These hallucinations are "harbingers and also signs of an immense spiritual power." A vision is actually "a higher excitation which adapts itself harmoniously to the most perfect health of mind and body." Complex hallucinations do not belong to the waking state but occur as a rule in a state of partial waking: the visionary is sunk in his vision to the point of complete absorption. Flournoy, too, was always able to establish "a certain degree of obnubilation" during the visions of Hélène Smith.[61] In our case the vision is complicated by a sleeping state whose peculiarities we shall discuss below.

The Change in Character

107   The most striking feature of the "second state" is the change in character. There are several cases in the literature which show this symptom of spontaneous change in the character of a person. The first to be made known in a scientific journal was that of Mary Reynolds, published by Weir Mitchell.[62] This was the case of a young woman living in Pennsylvania in 1811. After a deep sleep of about twenty hours, she had totally forgotten her entire past and everything she had ever learnt; even the words she spoke had lost their meaning. She no longer knew her relatives. Slowly she re-learnt to read and write, but her writing now was from right to left. More striking still was the change in her character. "Instead of being melancholy she was now cheerful to extremity. Instead of being reserved she was buoyant and social. Formerly taciturn and retiring, she was now

[59] "Des Hallucinations" (1845), as reviewed in *Allg Z f Psych*, IV (1848), p. 139.
[60] *Über Visionen*, pp. 285ff.
[61] Flournoy, p. 52.
[62] "Mary Reynolds: A Case of Double Consciousness" (1888). Also in *Harper's Magazine*, 1860. Abstracted *in extenso* in William James's *Principles of Psychology* (1891), pp. 391ff.

merry and jocose. Her disposition was totally and absolutely changed." [63]

08   In this state she gave up entirely her former secluded life and liked to set out on adventurous expeditions unarmed, through woods and mountains, on foot and on horseback. On one of these expeditions she encountered a large black bear, which she took for a pig. The bear stood up on his hind legs and gnashed his teeth at her. As she could not induce her horse to go any further, she went up to the bear with an ordinary stick and hit him until he took to flight. Five weeks later, after a deep sleep, she returned to her earlier state with amnesia for the interval. These states alternated for about sixteen years. But the last twenty-five years of her life Mary Reynolds passed exclusively in the second state.

09   Schroeder van der Kolk [64] reports the following case: The patient became ill at the age of sixteen with a periodic amnesia after a previous long illness of three years. Sometimes in the morning after waking she fell into a peculiar choreic state, during which she made rhythmical beating movements with her arms. Throughout the day she would behave in a childish, silly way, as if she had lost all her educated faculties. When normal she was very intelligent, well-read, spoke excellent French. In the second state she began to speak French faultily. On the second day she was always normal again. The two states were completely separated by amnesia.[65]

10   Höfelt [66] reports on a case of spontaneous somnambulism in a girl who in her normal state was submissive and modest, but in somnambulism was impertinent, rude, and violent. Azam's Felida [67] was in her normal state depressed, inhibited, timid, and in the second state lively, confident, enterprising to recklessness. The second state gradually became the dominant one and finally supplanted the first to such an extent that the patient called her normal states, which now lasted only a short time, her

63 Cf. Emminghaus, *Allgemeine Psychopathologie* (1878), p. 129, Ogier Ward's case.

64 *Pathologie und Therapie der Geisteskrankheiten* (1863), p. 31, quoted in *Allg Z f Psych*, XXII (1865), 406–7.

65 Cf. Donath, "Über Suggestibilität" (1892), quoted in *Arch f Psych u Nerv*, XXXII (1899), 335.

66 "Ein Fall von spontanem Somnambulismus" (1893).

67 *Hypnotisme* (1887), pp. 63ff.

"crises." The amnesic attacks had begun at the age of 14½. In time the second state became more moderate, and there was a certain approximation in the character of the two states. A very fine example of change in character is the case worked out by Camuset, Ribot, Legrand du Saule, Richer, and Voisin and put together by Bourru and Burot.[68] It is that of Louis V., a case of severe male hysteria, with an amnesic alternating character. In the first state he was rude, cheeky, querulous, greedy, thievish, inconsiderate. In the second state he showed an agreeable, sympathetic character and was industrious, docile, and obedient. The amnesic change in character has been put to literary use by Paul Lindau [69] in his play *Der Andere*. A case that parallels Lindau's criminalistic public prosecutor is reported on by Rieger.[70] The subconscious personalities of Janet's Lucie and Léonie,[71] or of Morton Prince's patient,[72] can also be regarded as parallels of our case, though these were artificial therapeutic products whose importance lies rather in the domain of dissociated consciousness and memory.

111   In all these cases the second state is separated from the first by an amnesic split, and the change in character is accompanied by a break in the continuity of consciousness. In our case there is no amnesic disturbance whatever; the transition from the first to the second state is quite gradual, continuity of consciousness is preserved, so that the patient carries over into the waking state everything she has experienced of the otherwise unknown regions of the unconscious during hallucinations in the second state.

112   Periodic changes in personality without an amnesic split are found in cyclic insanity, but they also occur as a rare phenomenon in hysteria, as Renaudin's case shows.[73] A young man, whose behaviour had always been exemplary, suddenly began to display the worst tendencies. No symptoms of insanity were observed, but on the other hand the whole surface of his body was found to be anaesthetic. This state was periodic, and, in the

---

68 *Variations de la personnalité* (1888).

69 See Moll, "Die Bewusstseinsspaltung in Paul Lindau's neuem Schauspiel" (1893), pp. 306ff.

70 *Der Hypnotismus* (1884), pp. 109ff.

71 *L'Automatisme psychologique.*

72 "An Experimental Study of Visions" (1898).

73 Quoted in Ribot, *Die Persönlichkeit* (1894).

same way, the patient's character was subject to fluctuations. As soon as the anaesthesia disappeared he became manageable and friendly. The moment it returned he was dominated by the worst impulses, including even the lust for murder.

113   If we remember that our patient's age at the beginning of the disturbances was 15½, i.e., that the age of puberty had just been reached, we must suppose that there was some connection between these disturbances and the physiological changes of character at puberty.

At this period of life there appears in the consciousness of the individual a new group of sensations together with the ideas and feelings arising therefrom. This continual pressure of unaccustomed mental states, which constantly make themselves felt because their cause is constantly at work, and which are co-ordinated with one another because they spring from one and the same source, must in the end bring about far-reaching changes in the constitution of the ego.[74]

We all know the fitful moods, the confused, new, powerful feelings, the tendency to romantic ideas, to exalted religiosity and mysticism, side by side with relapses into childishness, which give the adolescent his peculiar character. At this period he is making his first clumsy attempts at independence in every direction; for the first time he uses for his own purposes all that family and school have inculcated into him in childhood; he conceives ideals, constructs lofty plans for the future, lives in dreams whose main content is ambition and self-complacency. All this is physiological. The puberty of a psychopath is a serious crisis. Not only do the psychophysical changes run an exceedingly stormy course, but features of an inherited degenerate character, which do not appear in the child at all or only sporadically, now become fixed. In explaining our case we are bound to consider a specifically pubertal disturbance. The reasons for this will appear from a more detailed study of her second personality. For the sake of brevity we shall call this second personality Ivenes, as the patient herself christened her higher ego.

114   Ivenes is the direct continuation of her everyday ego. She comprises its whole conscious content. In the semi-somnambulist state her relation to the external world is analogous to that of the waking state—that is to say, she is influenced by re-

[74] Ribot, p. 69.

current hallucinations, but no more than persons who are subject to non-confusional psychotic hallucinations. The continuity of Ivenes obviously extends to the hysterical attacks as well, when she enacts dramatic scenes, has visionary experiences, etc. During the actual attack she is usually isolated from the external world, does not notice what is going on around her, does not know that she is talking loudly, etc. But she has no amnesia for the dream-content of the attack. Nor is there always amnesia for her motor expressions and for the changes in her surroundings. That this is dependent on the degree of somnambulistic stupor and on the partial paralysis of individual sense organs is proved by the occasion when the patient did not notice me, despite the fact that her eyes were open and that she probably saw the others, but only perceived my presence when I spoke to her. This is a case of so-called *systematic anaesthesia* (negative hallucination), which is frequently observed among hysterics.

115   Flournoy,[75] for instance, reports of Hélène Smith that during the séances she suddenly ceased to see those taking part, although she still heard their voices and felt their touch; or that she suddenly stopped hearing, although she saw the speakers moving their lips, etc.

116   Just as Ivenes is a continuation of the waking ego, so she carries over her whole conscious content into the waking state. This remarkable behaviour argues strongly against any analogy with cases of double consciousness. The characteristics reported of Ivenes contrast favourably with those of the patient; she is the calmer, more composed personality, and her pleasing modesty and reserve, her more uniform intelligence, her confident way of talking, may be regarded as an improvement on the patient's whole being; thus far there is some resemblance to Janet's Léonie. But it is no more than a resemblance. They are divided by a deep psychological difference, quite apart from the question of amnesia. Léonie II is the healthier, the more normal; she has regained her natural capacities, she represents the temporary amelioration of a chronic condition of hysteria. Ivenes gives more the impression of an artificial product; she is more contrived, and despite all her excellent points she strikes one as playing a part superlatively well. Her world-weariness, her longing for the Beyond, are not mere piety but the attributes

[75] *India to Mars*, p. 63.

of saintliness. Ivenes is no longer quite human, she is a mystic being who only half belongs to the world of reality. Her mournful features, her suffering resignation, her mysterious fate all lead us to the historical prototype of Ivenes: Justinus Kerner's Clairvoyante of Prevorst. I assume that the content of Kerner's book is generally known, so I omit references to the features they have in common. Ivenes, however, is not just a copy of the Clairvoyante; the latter is simply a sketch for an original. The patient pours her own soul into the role of the Clairvoyante, seeking to create out of it an ideal of virtue and perfection; she anticipates her own future and embodies in Ivenes what she wishes to be in twenty years' time—the assured, influential, wise, gracious, pious lady. In the construction of the second personality lies the deep-seated difference between Léonie II and Ivenes. Both are psychogenic, but whereas Léonie I obtains in Léonie II what properly belongs to her, the patient builds up a personality beyond herself. One cannot say that she deludes herself into the higher ideal state, rather she dreams herself into it.[76]

117   The realization of this dream is very reminiscent of the psychology of the pathological swindler. Delbrück[77] and Forel[78] have pointed out the importance of auto-suggestion in the development of pathological cheating and pathological daydreaming. Pick[79] regards intense auto-suggestion as the first symptom of hysterical dreamers which makes the realization of "daydreams" possible. One of Pick's patients dreamt herself into a morally dangerous situation and finally carried out an attempt at rape on herself by lying naked on the floor and tying herself to the table and chairs. The patients may create some dramatic personage with whom they enter into correspondence by letter,

[76] "[Somnambulistic dreams:] . . . romances of the subliminal imagination analogous to those 'continued stories' which so many people tell themselves in their moments of idleness, or at times when their routine occupations offer only slight obstacles to day-dreaming, and of which they themselves are generally the heroes. Fantastic constructions, taken up and pursued over and over again, but seldom seen through to the end, in which the imagination allows itself free play and revenges itself on the dull and drab matter-of-factness of everyday reality." Ibid., pp. 9f.

[77] *Die pathologische Lüge* (1891). [A reference in the 1953 edn. of *Two Essays on Analytical Psychology* (*Coll. Works*, 7), p. 134, n. 4, to this par. is in error. Instead see pars. 138ff., as indicated in the revised (1966) edn., p. 137, n. 3.—EDITORS.]

[78] *Hypnotism* (orig. 1889).

[79] "Über pathologische Träumerei" (1896), pp. 280–301.

as in Bohn's case,[80] where the patient dreamt herself into an engagement with a completely imaginary lawyer in Nice, from whom she received letters which she had written herself in disguised handwriting. This pathological dreaming, with its auto-suggestive falsifications of memory sometimes amounting to actual delusions and hallucinations, is also found in the lives of many saints.[81] It is only a step from dreamy ideas with a strong sensuous colouring to complex hallucinations proper.[82] For instance, in Pick's first case, one can see how the patient, who imagined she was the Empress Elizabeth, gradually lost herself in her reveries to such an extent that her condition must be regarded as a true twilight state. Later it passed over into an hysterical delirium in which her dream fantasies became typical hallucinations. The pathological liar who lets himself be swept away by his fantasies behaves exactly like a child who loses himself in the game he is playing,[83] or like an actor who surrenders completely to his part. There is no fundamental distinction between this and the somnambulistic dissociation of the personality, but only a difference of degree based on the intensity of the primary auto-suggestibility or disaggregation of the psychic elements. The more consciousness becomes dissociated the greater becomes the plasticity of the dream situations, and the less, too, the amount of conscious lying and of consciousness in general. This state of being carried away by one's interest in the object is what Freud calls hysterical identification. For instance, Erler's patient,[84] a severe hysteric, had hypnagogic visions of little riders made of paper, who so took possession of her imagination that she had the feeling of being herself one of them. Much the same sort of thing normally happens to us in dreams, when we cannot help thinking "hysterically." [85] Complete surrender to the interesting idea explains the wonderful

[80] Ein Fall von doppeltem Bewusstsein (1898).
[81] Görres, Die christliche Mystik (1836–42).
[82] Cf. Behr, "Erinnerungsfälschungen und pathologische Traumzustände" (1899), pp. 918ff.; also Ballet, Le Langage intérieur, p. 44.
[83] Cf. Redlich, "Pseudologia phantastica" (1900), p. 66.
[84] "Hysterisches und hystero-epileptisches Irresein" (1879), p. 21.
[85] Binet, p. 89: "I may say in this connection that hysterical patients have been my chosen subjects, because they exaggerate the phenomena that must necessarily be found to some degree in many persons who have never shown hysterical symptoms."

naturalness of these pseudological or somnambulistic performances, which is quite beyond the reach of conscious acting. The
less the waking consciousness intervenes with its reflection and
calculation, the more certain and convincing becomes the objectivation of the dream.[86]

118   Our case has still another analogy with *pseudologia phantastica*: the development of fantasies during the attacks. Many
cases are known in the literature of fits of pathological lying,
accompanied by various hysteriform complaints.[87] Our patient
develops her fantasy systems exclusively during the attack. In
her normal state she is quite incapable of thinking out new
ideas or explanations; she must either put herself into the
somnambulistic state or await its spontaneous appearance. This
exhausts the affinities with *pseudologia phantastica* and pathological dreaming.

119   Our patient differs essentially from pathological dreamers
in that it could never be proved that her reveries had previously
been the object of her daily interests; her dreams came up ex-
plosively, suddenly bursting forth with amazing completeness
from the darkness of the unconscious. The same thing happened with Flournoy's Hélène Smith. At several points, however, it is possible in our case to demonstrate the link with
perceptions in the normal state [see next par.], so it seems probable that the roots of those dreams were originally feeling-toned
ideas which only occupied her waking consciousness for a short
time.[88] We must suppose that hysterical forgetfulness [89] plays

86 As, for instance, in the roof-climbing of somnambulists.

87 Delbrück, *Die Lüge;* and Redlich, op. cit. Cf. also the development of delusional ideas in epileptic twilight states mentioned by Mörchen, *Über Dämmerzustände* (1901), pp. 51, 59.

88 Cf. Flournoy's interesting conjecture as to the origin of H. S.'s Hindu cycle:
"I should not be surprised if Marlès' remark on the beauty of the Kanara women
were the sting, the tiny jab, which aroused the subliminal attention and riveted
it, quite naturally, on this single passage and the two or three lines that followed it, to the exclusion of all the much less interesting context" (Swiss edn.,
p. 285).

89 Janet says (*The Mental State of Hystericals,* orig. 1893, p. 78); "It is from
forgetfulness that there arise, not always, but very often, the supposed lies of
hysterical subjects. In the same way we can also explain their caprices, their
changes of mood, their ingratitude, in a word their inconsistencies, for the connection of the past with the present, which gives seriousness and unity to conduct, depends largely upon memory."

a not inconsiderable role in the origin of such dreams: many ideas which, in themselves, would be worth preserving in consciousness, sink below the threshold, associated trains of thought get lost and, thanks to psychic dissociation, go on working in the unconscious. We meet the same process again in the genesis of our own dreams.[90] The apparently sudden and unexpected reveries of the patient can be explained in this way. The total submersion of the conscious personality in the dream role is also the indirect cause of the development of simultaneous automatisms:

A second condition may also occasion the division of consciousness. It is not an alteration of sensibility, but it is rather a peculiar attitude of the mind—the concentration of attention on a single thing. The result of this state of concentration is that the mind is absorbed to the exclusion of other things, and to such a degree insensible that the way is opened for automatic actions; and these actions, becoming more complicated, as in the preceding case, may assume a psychic character and constitute intelligences of a parasitic kind, existing side by side with the normal personality, which is not aware of them.[91]

120   Our patient's "romances" throw a most significant light on the subjective roots of her dreams. They swarm with open and secret love-affairs, with illegitimate births and other sexual innuendoes. The hub of all these ambiguous stories is a lady whom she dislikes, and who gradually turns into her polar opposite, for whereas Ivenes is the pinnacle of virtue this lady is a sink of iniquity. But the patient's reincarnation theory, in which she appears as the ancestral mother of countless thousands, springs, in all of its naïve nakedness, straight from an

---

[90] Cf. Freud, *The Interpretation of Dreams*, p. 593: "The course of our conscious reflections shows us that we follow a particular path in our application of attention. If, as we follow this path, we come upon an idea which will not bear criticism, we break off: we drop the cathexis of attention. Now it seems that the train of thought which has thus been initiated and dropped can continue to spin itself out without attention being turned to it again, unless at some point or other it reaches a specially high degree of intensity which forces attention to it. Thus, if a train of thought is initially rejected (consciously, perhaps) by a judgment that it is wrong or that it is useless for the immediate intellectual purposes in view, the result may be that this train of thought will proceed, unobserved by consciousness, until the onset of sleep."
[91] Binet, *Alterations*, pp. 93f., modified.

exuberant fantasy which is so very characteristic of the puberty period. It is the woman's premonition of sexual feeling, the dream of fertility, that has created these monstrous ideas in the patient. We shall not be wrong if we seek the main cause of this curious clinical picture in her budding sexuality. From this point of view the whole essence of Ivenes and her enormous family is nothing but a dream of sexual wish-fulfilment, which differs from the dream of a night only in that it is spread over months and years.

[*Nature of the Somnambulistic Attacks*]

21   So far there is one point in S. W.'s history that has not been discussed, and that is the nature of her attacks. In the second séance she was suddenly seized with a sort of fainting-fit, from which she awoke with a recollection of various hallucinations. According to her own statement, she had not lost consciousness for a moment. Judging from the outward symptoms and course of these attacks, one is inclined to think of narcolepsy or lethargy, of the kind described, for instance, by Loewenfeld. This is the more plausible since we know that one member of her family—the grandmother—had once had an attack of lethargy. So it is conceivable that our patient inherited the lethargic disposition (Loewenfeld). One often observes hysterical fits of convulsions at spiritualistic séances. Our patient never showed any symptoms of convulsions, but instead she had those peculiar sleeping states. Aetiologically, two elements must be considered for the first attack:

(1) The influence of hypnosis.
(2) Psychic excitation.

22   (1) INFLUENCE OF PARTIAL HYPNOSIS. Janet observed that subconscious automatisms have a hypnotic influence and can bring about complete somnambulism.[92] He made the following experiment: While the patient, who was fully awake, was engaged in conversation by a second observer, Janet stationed him-

---

92 *L'Automatisme psychologique*, p. 329: "Another consideration emphasizes the resemblance between these two states, namely, that subconscious acts have a kind of hypnotizing effect, and one that helps by their very performance to induce somnambulism."

self behind her and by means of whispered suggestions made her unconsciously move her hand, write, and answer questions by signs. Suddenly the patient broke off the conversation, turned round, and with supraliminal consciousness continued the previously subconscious talk with Janet. She had fallen into hypnotic somnambulism.[93] In this example we see a process similar to our case. But, for certain reasons to be discussed later, the sleeping state cannot be regarded as hypnotic. We therefore come to the question of:

123   (2) PSYCHIC EXCITATION. It is reported that the first time Bettina Brentano met Goethe, she suddenly fell asleep on his knee.[94] Ecstatic sleep in the midst of extreme torture, the so-called "witch's sleep," is a well-known phenomenon in the annals of witchcraft.[95]

124   With susceptible subjects, comparatively small stimuli are enough to induce somnambulistic states. For example, a sensitive lady had to have a splinter cut out of her finger. Without any kind of bodily change she suddenly saw herself sitting beside a brook in a beautiful meadow, plucking flowers. This condition lasted all through the minor operation and then vanished without having any special after-effects.[96]

125   Loewenfeld observed the unintentional induction of hysterical lethargy by hypnosis.[97] Our case has certain resemblances to hysterical lethargy as described by Loewenfeld: [98] superficial respiration, lowering of the pulse, corpse-like pallor of the face, also peculiar feelings of dying and thoughts of death.[99] Retention of one or more senses is no argument against lethargy: for instance in certain cases of apparent death the sense of hearing remains.[100] In Bonamaison's case,[101] not only was the sense of

93 Ibid., p. 329.

94 Gustave Flaubert made literary use of this falling asleep at the moment of supreme excitement in his novel *Salammbô*. When the hero, after many struggles, at last captures Salammbô, he suddenly falls asleep just as he touches her virginal bosom.

95 Cases of emotional paralysis may also come into this category. Cf. Baetz, "Über Emotionslähmung" (1901), pp. 717ff.

96 Hagen, "Zur Theorie der Hallucination" (1868), p. 17.

97 "Über hysterische Schlafzustände" (1892), p. 59.

98 Cf. Flournoy, *India to Mars*, pp. 67f.

99 Loewenfeld (1891), p. 737.

100 Ibid., p. 734.

101 "Un Cas remarquable d'hypnose spontanée" (1890), p. 234.

touch retained, but the senses of hearing and smell were sharpened. Hallucinations and loud speaking of hallucinatory persons are also met with in lethargy.[102] As a rule there is total amnesia for the lethargic interval. Loewenfeld's case D. had a vague memory afterwards,[103] and in Bonamaison's case there was no amnesia. Lethargic patients do not prove accessible to the usual stimuli for rousing them, but Loewenfeld succeeded, with his patient St., in changing the lethargy into hypnosis by means of mesmeric passes, thus establishing contact with the rest of her consciousness during the attack.[104] Our patient proved at first absolutely inaccessible during lethargy; later she started to speak spontaneously, was indistractible when her somnambulistic ego was speaking, but distractible when the speaker was one of her automatic personalities. In the latter case, it seems probable that the hypnotic effect of the automatisms succeeded in achieving a partial transformation of the lethargy into hypnosis. When we consider Loewenfeld's view that the lethargic disposition must not be "identified outright with the peculiar behaviour of the nervous apparatus in hysteria," then the assumption that this disposition was due to family heredity becomes fairly probable. The clinical picture is much complicated by these attacks.

126   So far we have seen that the patient's ego-consciousness was identical in all states. We have discussed two secondary complexes of consciousness and followed them into the somnambulistic attack, where, owing to loss of motor expression, they appeared to the patient in the second séance as a vision of the two grandfathers. These complexes completely disappeared from view during the attacks that followed, but on the other hand they developed an all the more intense activity during the twilight state, in the form of visions. It seems that numerous secondary sequences of ideas must have split off quite early from the primary unconscious personality, for soon after the first two séances "spirits" appeared by the dozen. The names were inexhaustible in their variety, but the differences between the various personalities were exhausted very quickly, and it became apparent that they could all be classified under two

102 Loewenfeld (1891), p. 737.
103 Ibid., p. 737.
104 Loewenfeld (1892), pp. 59ff.

types, the *serio-religious* and the *gay-hilarious*. It was really only a question of two different subconscious personalities appearing under various names, which had however no essential significance. The older type, the grandfather, who had started the automatisms off in the first place, was also the first to make use of the twilight state. I cannot remember any suggestion that might have given rise to the automatic speaking. According to our previous explanations, the attack can in these circumstances be thought of as a partial self-hypnosis. The ego-consciousness which remains over and, as a result of its isolation from the external world, occupies itself entirely with its hallucinations, is all that is left of the waking consciousness. Thus the automatism has a wide field for its activity. The autonomy of the individual centres, which we found to be present in the patient from the beginning, makes the act of automatic speaking more understandable. Dreamers, too, occasionally talk in their sleep, and people in the waking state sometimes accompany intense thought with unconscious whispering.[105] The peculiar movements of the speech muscles are worth noting. They have also been observed in other somnambulists.[106] These clumsy attempts can be directly paralleled by the unintelligent and clumsy movements of the table or glass; in all probability they correspond to the preliminary expression of the motor components of an idea, or they correspond to an excitation limited to the motor centres and not yet subordinated to a higher system. I do not know whether anything of the sort occurs with people who talk in their dreams, but it has been observed in hypnotized persons.[107]

127   Since the convenient medium of speech was used as the means of communication, it made the study of the subconscious personalities considerably easier. Their intellectual range was relatively narrow. Their knowledge comprised all that the patient knew in her waking state, plus a few incidental details

[105] Cf. Lehmann's researches into involuntary whispering, in *Aberglaube und Zauberei* (1898), pp. 386ff.

[106] Flournoy, for instance, writes (p. 103): "In a first attempt, Leopold [H. S.'s control] only succeeded in giving Hélène his intonation and pronunciation; after a séance in which she suffered acutely in her mouth and in her neck, as though her vocal organs were being manipulated or removed, she began to talk in a natural voice."

[107] Loewenfeld (1892), p. 60.

such as the birthdays of unknown persons who were dead, etc. The source of this information is rather obscure, since the patient did not know how she could have procured knowledge of these facts in the ordinary way. They were cryptomnesias, but are too insignificant to deserve more detailed mention. The two subconscious personalities had a very meagre intelligence; they produced almost nothing but banalities. The interesting thing is their relation to the ego-consciousness of the patient in the somnambulistic state. They were well informed about everything that took place during the ecstasies and occasionally gave an exact report, like a running commentary.[108] But they had only a very superficial knowledge of the patient's fantasies; they did not understand them and were unable to answer a single question on this subject correctly; their stereotyped reply was "Ask Ivenes." This observation reveals a dualism in the nature of the subconscious personalities which is rather difficult to explain; for the grandfather, who manifests himself through automatic speech, also appears to Ivenes, and according to her own statement "knew all her thoughts." How is it that when the grandfather speaks through the mouth of the patient he knows nothing about the very things he teaches Ivenes in the ecstasies?

128   Let us go back to what we said at the first appearance of the hallucinations [par. 98]. There we described the vision of the grandfathers as an irruption of hypnosis into the visual sphere. That irruption did not lead to a "normal" hypnosis but to "hystero-hypnosis"; in other words, the simple hypnosis was complicated by an hysterical attack.

129   It is not a rare occurrence for normal hypnosis to be disturbed, or rather to be replaced, by the unexpected appearance of hysterical somnambulism; the hypnotist in many cases then loses rapport with the patient. In our case the automatism arising in the motor area plays the part of the hypnotist, and the suggestions emanating from it (objectively described as autosuggestions) hypnotize the neighbouring areas which have grown susceptible. But the moment the hypnosis affects the visual

108 This reminds us of Flournoy's observations: while H. S. speaks somnambulistically as Marie Antoinette, her arms do not belong to the somnambulistic personality but to the automatist Leopold, who converses by gestures with the observer. Cf. Flournoy, pp. 130f.

sphere the hysterical attack intervenes, and this, as we have remarked, effects a very profound change over large portions of the psychic area. We must picture the automatism as standing in the same relation to the attack as the hypnotist to a pathological hypnosis: it loses its influence on the subsequent development of the situation. The hallucinatory appearance of the hypnotic personality, or of the suggested idea, may be regarded as its last effect on the personality of the somnambulist. Thereafter the hypnotist becomes a mere figure with whom the somnambulistic personality engages autonomously; he can only just make out what is going on, but can no longer condition the content of the attack. The autonomous ego-complex—in this case Ivenes—now has the upper hand, and she groups her own mental products around the personality of her hypnotist, the grandfather, now diminished to a mere image. In this way we are able to understand the dualism in the nature of the grandfather. *Grandfather I, who speaks directly to those present, is a totally different person and a mere spectator of his double, Grandfather II, who appears as Ivenes' teacher.* Grandfather I maintains energetically that both are one and the same person, that Grandfather I has all the knowledge which Grandfather II possesses and is only prevented from making it public because of language difficulties. (The patient herself was naturally not conscious of this split, but took both to be the same person.) On closer inspection, however, Grandfather I is not altogether wrong, and he can appeal to an observation which apparently confirms the identity of I and II, i.e., the fact that they are never both present together, When I is speaking automatically, II is not present, and Ivenes remarks on his absence. Similarly, during her ecstasies, when she is with II, she cannot say where I is, or she only learns on returning from her journeys that he has been guarding her body in the meantime. Conversely, the grandfather never speaks when he is going on a journey with Ivenes or when he gives her special illumination. This behaviour is certainly remarkable, for if Grandfather I is the hypnotist and completely separate from the personality of Ivenes, there seems no reason why he should not speak objectively at the same time that his double appears in the ecstasy. Although this might have been supposed possible, as a matter of fact it was never observed. How is this dilemma to be resolved? Sure enough there is an identity of I and II, but it does not lie in the realm of the personality under discussion; it lies rather in the basis common to both, namely in the personality of the patient, which is in the deepest sense one and indivisible.

130   Here we come upon the characteristic feature of all hysterical splits of consciousness. They are disturbances that only touch the surface, and none of them goes so deep as to attack the firmly knit basis of the ego-complex. Somewhere, often in an extremely well-concealed place, we find the bridge which spans the apparently impassable abyss. For instance, one of four playing cards is made invisible to a hypnotized person by suggestion; consequently he calls only the other three. A pencil is then put into his hand and he is told to write down all the cards before him; he correctly adds the fourth one.[109] Again, a patient of Janet's [110] always saw, in the aura of his hystero-epileptic attacks, the vision of a conflagration. Whenever he saw an open fire he had an attack; indeed, the sight of a lighted match held before him was sufficient to induce one. The patient's visual field was limited to 30° on the left side; the right eye was closed. The left eye was then focused on the centre of a perimeter while a lighted match was held at 80°. An hystero-epileptic attack took place immediately. Despite extensive amnesia in many cases of double consciousness, the patients do not behave in a way that corresponds to the degree of their ignorance, but as though some obscure instinct still guided their actions in accordance with their former knowledge. Neither this relatively mild amnesic split nor even the severe amnesia of the epileptic twilight state, formerly regarded as an *irreparabile damnum*, is sufficient to sever the innermost threads that bind the ego-complex of the twilight state to that of the normal state. In one case it was possible to articulate the content of the twilight state with the waking ego-complex.[111]

131   If we apply these discoveries to our case, we arrive at the explanatory hypothesis that, under the influence of appropriate suggestions, the layers of the unconscious which are beyond reach of the split try to represent the unity of the automatic

---

[109] Dessoir, *Das Doppel-Ich* (1896), p. 29.
[110] Janet, "L'Anesthésie hystérique," p. 69.
[111] Graeter, "Ein Fall von epileptischer Amnesie durch Hypermnesie beseitigt" (1899), p. 129.

personality, but that this endeavour comes to grief on the profounder and more elementary disturbance caused by the hysterical attack.[112] This prevents a more complete synthesis by appending associations which are, as it were, the truest and most original property of the "supraconscious" personality. The dream of Ivenes, as it emerges into consciousness, is put into the mouths of the figures who happen to be in the field of vision, and henceforth it remains associated with these persons.

[Origin of the Unconscious Personalities]

132   As we have seen, the various personalities are grouped round two types, the grandfather and Ulrich von Gerbenstein. The grandfather produces nothing but sanctimonious twaddle and edifying moral precepts. Ulrich von Gerbenstein is simply a silly schoolgirl, with nothing masculine about him except his name. We must here add, from the anamnesis, that the patient was confirmed at the age of fifteen by a very pietistic clergyman, and that even at home she had to listen to moral sermons. The grandfather represents this side of her past, Gerbenstein the other half; hence the curious contrast. So here we have, personified, the chief characters of the past: here the compulsorily educated bigot, there the boisterousness of a lively girl of fifteen who often goes too far.[113] The patient herself is a peculiar mixture of both; sometimes timid, shy, excessively reserved, at other times boisterous to the point of indecency. She is often painfully conscious of these contrasts. This gives us the key to the origin of the two subconscious personalities. The patient is obviously seeking a middle way between two extremes; she endeavours to repress them and strives for a more ideal state. These strivings lead to the adolescent dream of the ideal Ivenes, beside whom the unrefined aspects of her character fade into the background. They are not lost; but as repressed thoughts,

---

[112] Karplus, "Über Pupillenstarre im hysterischen Anfall" (1898), p. 52, says: "The hysterical attack is not a purely psychic process. . . . The psychic processes merely release a pre-existing mechanism, which in itself has nothing to do with them."

[113] This objectivation of associated complexes has been used by Carl Hauptmann in his play Die Bergschmiede (1902), where the treasure-seeker is confronted one gloomy night by the hallucination of his entire better self.

analogous to the idea of Ivenes, they begin to lead an independent existence as autonomous personalities.

133   This behaviour calls to mind Freud's dream investigations, which disclose the independent growth of repressed thoughts.[114] We can now understand why the hallucinatory persons are divorced from those who write and speak automatically. They teach Ivenes the secrets of the Beyond, they tell her all those fantastic stories about the extraordinariness of her personality, they create situations in which she can appear dramatically with the attributes of their power, wisdom, and virtue. They are nothing but dramatized split-offs from her dream-ego. The others, the automata, are the ones to be overcome; they must have no part in Ivenes. The only thing they have in common with her spirit companions is the name. It is not to be expected in a case like this, where no clear-cut divisions exist, that two such pregnant groups of characters, with all their idiosyncrasies, should disappear entirely from a somnambulistic ego-complex so closely connected with the waking consciousness. And in fact, we meet them again, partly in those ecstatic penitential scenes and partly in the romances that are crammed with more or less banal, mischievous gossip. On the whole, however, a very much milder form predominates.

Course of the Disorder

134   It only remains now to say a few words about the course of this singular ailment. The whole process reached its climax within four to eight weeks, and the descriptions of Ivenes and the other subconscious personalities refer in general to this period. Thereafter a gradual decline became noticeable; the ecstasies grew more and more vacuous as Gerbenstein's influence increased. The phenomena lost their plasticity and became ever shallower; characters which at first were well differentiated became by degrees inextricably mixed. The psychological yield grew more and more meagre, until finally the whole story assumed the appearance of a first-class fraud. Ivenes herself was severely hit by this decline; she became painfully uncertain, spoke cautiously, as if feeling her way, so that the character of

114 *The Interpretation of Dreams.* Cf. also Breuer and Freud, *Studies on Hysteria* (orig. 1895).

the patient came through in more and more undisguised form. The somnambulistic attacks, too, decreased in frequency and intensity. One could observe with one's own eyes all the gradations from somnambulism to conscious lying.

135   Thus the curtain fell. The patient has since gone abroad. The fact that her character has become pleasanter and more stable may have a significance that is not to be underestimated, if we remember those cases where the second state gradually came to replace the first. We may be dealing here with a similar phenomenon.

136   It is well known that somnambulistic symptoms are particularly common in puberty.[115] The attacks of somnambulism in Dyce's case[116] began immediately before the onset of puberty and lasted just till its end. The somnambulism of Hélène Smith is likewise closely connected with puberty.[117] Schroeder van der Kolk's patient was 16 at the time of her illness; Felida X., $14\frac{1}{2}$. We know also that the future character is formed and fixed at this period. We saw in the cases of Felida X. and Mary Reynolds how the character of the second state gradually replaced that of the first. It is, therefore, conceivable that the phenomena of double consciousness are simply new character formations, or attempts of the future personality to break through, and that in consequence of special difficulties (unfavourable circumstances, psychopathic disposition of the nervous system, etc.) they get bound up with peculiar disturbances of consciousness. In view of the difficulties that oppose the future character, the somnambulisms sometimes have an eminently teleological significance, in that they give the individual, who would otherwise inevitably succumb, the means of victory. Here I am thinking especially of Joan of Arc, whose extraordinary courage reminds one of the feats performed by Mary Reynolds in her second state. This is also, perhaps, the place to point out the like significance of "teleological hallucinations," of which occasional cases come to the knowledge of the public, although they have not yet been subjected to scientific study.

115 Pelman, "Über das Verhalten des Gedächtnisses bei den verschiedenen Formen des Irreseins" (1864), p. 74.
116 Jessen, "Doppeltes Bewusstsein" (1865), p. 407.
117 Flournoy, p. 31.

Heightened Unconscious Performance

137   We have now discussed all the essential phenomena presented by our case which were significant for its inner structure.
Certain accompanying phenomena have still to be briefly considered; these are the phenomena of *heightened unconscious
performance*. In this field, we meet with a not altogether un-
justifiable scepticism on the part of the scientific pundits. Even
Dessoir's conception of the second ego aroused considerable
opposition and was rejected in many quarters as too enthusias-
tic. As we know, occultism has claimed a special right to this
field and has drawn premature conclusions from dubious observations. We are still very far indeed from being able to say
anything conclusive, for up to the present our material is nothing like adequate. If, therefore, we touch on this question of
heightened unconscious performance, we do so only to do justice to all sides of our case.

138   By heightened unconscious performance we mean that peculiar automatic process whose results are not available for the
conscious psychic activity of the individual. Under this category
comes, first of all, thought-reading by means of table movements. I do not know whether there are people who can guess
an entire long train of thought by means of inductive inferences
from the "intended tremors." At any rate it is certain that,
granting this to be possible, such persons must be making use
of a routine acquired by endless practice. But in our case routine can be ruled out at once, and there is no choice but to
assume for the present a receptivity of the unconscious far ex-
ceeding that of the conscious mind. This assumption is supported by numerous observations on somnambulists. Here I
will mention only Binet's experiments, where little letters or
other small objects, or complicated little figures in relief, were
laid on the anaesthesic skin of the back of the hand or the neck,
and the unconscious perceptions were registered by means of
signs. On the basis of these experiments he comes to the following conclusion: "According to the calculations that I have been
able to make, the unconscious sensibility of an hysterical patient is at certain moments *fifty times* more acute than that of

a normal person." [118] Another example of heightened performance that applies to our case and to numerous other somnambulists is the process known as cryptomnesia.[119] By this is meant the coming into consciousness of a memory-image which is not recognized as such in the first instance, but only secondarily, if at all, by means of subsequent recollection or abstract reasoning. It is characteristic of cryptomnesia that the image which comes up does not bear the distinctive marks of the memory-image—that is to say, it is not connected with the supraliminal ego-complex in question.

139   There are three different ways in which the cryptomnesic image may be brought into consciousness:

(1) *The image enters consciousness without the mediation of the senses, intrapsychically.* It is a sudden idea or hunch, whose causal nexus is hidden from the person concerned. To this extent cryptomnesia is an everyday occurrence and is intimately bound up with normal psychic processes. But how often it misleads the scientist, author, or composer into believing that his ideas are original, and then along comes the critic and points out the source! Generally the individual formulation of the idea protects the author from the charge of plagiarism and proves his good faith, though there are cases where the reproduction occurs unconsciously, almost word for word. Should the passage contain a remarkable idea, then the suspicion of more or less conscious plagiarism is justified. After all, an important idea is linked by numerous associations to the ego-complex; it has been thought about at different times and in different situations and therefore has innumerable connecting threads leading in all directions. Consequently it can never disappear so entirely from consciousness that its continuity is lost to the sphere of conscious memory. We have, however, a criterion by which we can always recognize intrapsychic cryptomnesia objectively: the cryptomnesic idea is linked to the ego-complex by the minimum of associations. The reason for this lies in the relation of the individual to the object concerned, in the want of proportion between interest and object.

118 *Alterations*, p. 139.

119 Cryptomnesia should not be confused with hypermnesia. By the latter term is meant the abnormal sharpening of the powers of memory, which then reproduce the actual memory-images themselves.

Two possibilities are conceivable: (*a*) The object is worthy of interest, but the interest is slight owing to distractibility or lack of understanding. (*b*) The object is not worthy of interest, consequently the interest is slight. In both cases there is an extremely labile connection with consciousness, the result being that the object is quickly forgotten. This flimsy bridge soon breaks down and the idea sinks into the unconscious, where it is no longer accessible to the conscious mind. Should it now re-enter consciousness by way of cryptomnesia, the feeling of strangeness, of its being an original creation, will cling to it, because the path by which it entered the subconscious can no longer be discovered. Strangeness and original creation are, moreover, closely allied to one another, if we remember the numerous witnesses in *belles-lettres* to the "possessed" nature of genius.[120] Apart from a number of striking instances of this kind, where it is doubtful whether it is cryptomnesia or an original creation, there are others where a passage of no essential value has been reproduced cryptomnesically, and in almost the same words, as in the following example:

40 Nietzsche, *Thus Spake Zara-thustra* [121]

Kerner, *Blätter aus Prevorst* [122]

Now about the time that Zarathustra sojourned on the Happy Isles, it happened that a ship anchored at the isle on which

The four captains and a merchant, Mr. Bell, went ashore on the island of Mount Stromboli to shoot rabbits. At three o'clock

120 Cf. Nietzsche, *Ecce Homo* (trans. by Ludovici), pp. 101f.: "Has any one at the end of the nineteenth century any distinct notion of what poets of a stronger age understood by the word 'inspiration'? If not, I will describe it. If one had the smallest vestige of superstition left in one, it would hardly be possible completely to set aside the idea that one is the mere incarnation, mouthpiece, or medium of an almighty power. The idea of revelation, in the sense that something which profoundly convulses and upsets one becomes suddenly visible and audible with indescribable certainty and accuracy, describes the simple fact. One hears—one does not seek; one takes—one does not ask who gives; a thought suddenly flashes up like lightning, it comes with necessity, without faltering—I have never had any choice in the matter."

121 Ch. XL, "Great Events" (trans. by Common, p. 180, slightly modified). (Orig. 1883.)

122 Vol. IV, p. 57, headed: "An Extract of Awe-Inspiring Import from the Log of the Ship *Sphinx* in the Year 1686, in the Mediterranean." (Orig. 1831–39.) [Cf. "Cryptomnesia," par. 181, in C.W. 1.—EDITORS.]

the smoking mountain stands, and the crew went ashore to shoot rabbits. About the noontide hour, however, when the captain and his men were together again, they suddenly saw a man coming towards them through the air, and a voice said distinctly: "It is time! It is highest time!" But when the figure drew close to them, flying past quickly like a shadow in the direction of the volcano, they recognized with the greatest dismay that it was Zarathustra. . . . "Behold," said the old helmsman, "Zarathustra goes down to hell!"

they mustered the crew to go aboard, when, to their inexpressible astonishment, they saw two men flying rapidly towards them through the air. One was dressed in black, the other in grey. They came past them very closely, in the greatest haste, and to their utmost dismay descended amid the burning flames into the crater of the terrible volcano, Mount Stromboli. They recognized the pair as acquaintances from London.

141   Nietzsche's sister, Elisabeth Förster-Nietzsche, told me, in reply to my enquiry, that Nietzsche had taken a lively interest in Kerner when staying with his grandfather, Pastor Oehler, in Pobler, between the ages of 12 and 15, but certainly not later. It could scarcely have been Nietzsche's intention to commit a plagiarism from a ship's log; had this been the case he would surely have omitted that extremely prosaic and totally irrelevant passage about shooting rabbits. Obviously, when painting the picture of Zarathustra's descent into hell, that forgotten impression from his youth must have slipped half or wholly unconsciously into his mind.

142   This example shows all the peculiarities of cryptomnesia: a quite unimportant detail which only deserves to be forgotten as quickly as possible is suddenly reproduced with almost literal fidelity, while the main point of the story is, one cannot say modified, but re-created in an individual manner. Around the individual core—the idea of the journey to hell—there are deposited, as picturesque details, those old, forgotten impressions of a similar situation. The story itself is so absurd that the young Nietzsche, a voracious reader, probably skimmed through it without evincing any very profound interest in the matter. Here, then, is the required minimum of associative connections,

86

for we can hardly conceive of a greater jump than from that stupid old tale to Nietzsche's consciousness in the year 1883. If we realize Nietzsche's state of mind [123] at the time when he wrote *Zarathustra,* and the poetic ecstasy that at more than one point verges on the pathological, this abnormal reminiscence will appear more understandable.

143 The other of the two possibilities mentioned above, namely, registering some object, not in itself uninteresting, in a state of distractibility or partial interest due to lack of understanding, and its cryptomnesic reproduction, is found mainly in somnambulists, and also—as curiosities of literature—in people at the point of death.[124] Out of the rich choice of these phenomena we are chiefly concerned here with speaking in foreign tongues, the symptom of glossolalia. This phenomenon is mentioned in practically all cases of ecstasy; it is found in the New Testament, in the *Acta Sanctorum,*[125] in the witch trials, and in recent times in the story of the Clairvoyante of Prevorst, in Judge Edmond's daughter Laura, in Flournoy's Hélène Smith, who was thoroughly investigated on this question too, and also in Bresler's case,[126] which was probably identical with that of Blumhardt's Gottliebin Dittus.[127] As Flournoy has shown, glossolalia, in so far as it is a really independent language, is a cryptomnesic phenomenon par excellence. I would refer the reader to Flournoy's exceedingly interesting study of this subject.[128]

144 In our case glossolalia was observed only once, and then the only intelligible words were the interspersed variations of the word *vena.* The origin of this word is clear: a few days previously the patient had dipped into an anatomical atlas and immersed herself in a study of the veins of the face, which were

123 In *Ecce Homo:* "There is an ecstasy so great that the tremendous strain of it is at times eased by a storm of tears, when your steps now involuntarily rush ahead, now lag behind; a feeling of being completely beside yourself, with the most distinct consciousness of innumerable delicate thrills tingling through you to your very toes; a depth of happiness, in which pain and gloom do not act as its antitheses, but as its condition, as a challenge, as necessary shades of colour in such an excess of light." [Cf. Ludovici trans., p. 102.]

124 Eckermann, *Conversations with Goethe,* p. 587.

125 Cf. Görres, *Die christliche Mystik.*

126 "Kulturhistorischer Beitrag zur Hysterie" (1896), pp. 333ff.

127 Zündel, *Pfarrer J. C. Blumhardt* (1880).

128 *From India to the Planet Mars.*

given in Latin, and she used the word *vena* in her dreams, just as a normal person might do. The remaining words and sentences in foreign language reveal at a glance their derivation from the patient's slight knowledge of French. Unfortunately I did not get exact translations of the various sentences, because the patient refused to give them to me; but we can take it that it was the same sort of thing as Hélène Smith's Martian language. Flournoy shows that this Martian language was nothing but a childish translation from the French; only the words were altered, the syntax remained the same. A more probable explanation is that our patient simply strung a lot of meaningless foreign-sounding words together, and, instead of forming any true words,[129] borrowed certain characteristic sounds from French and Italian and combined them into a sort of language, just as Hélène Smith filled in the gaps between the real Sanskrit words with pseudo-linguistic products of her own. The curious names of the mystical system can mostly be traced back to known roots. Even the circles remind one of the planetary orbits found in every school atlas; the inner parallel with the relation of the planets to the sun is also pretty clear, so we shall not go far wrong if we see the names as reminiscences of popular astronomy. In this way the names "Persus," "Fenus," "Nenus," "Sirum," "Surus," "Fixus," and "Pix" can be explained as childish distortions of "Perseus," "Venus," "Sirius," and "fixed star," analogous to the *vena* variations. "Magnesor" is reminiscent of "magnetism," whose mystical significance the patient knew from the Clairvoyante of Prevorst story. "Connesor" being contrary to "Magnesor," the first syllable "Con-" suggests French "contre." "Hypos" and "Hyfonism" remind one of "hypnosis" and "hypnotism," about which the weirdest ideas still circulate amongst laymen. The frequent endings in "-us" and "-os" are the signs by which most people distinguish between Latin and Greek. The other names derive from similar accidents to which we lack the clues. Naturally the modest glossolalia of our case cannot claim to be a classic example of cryptomnesia, for it con-

---

[129] ". . . the rapid and confused gibberish whose meaning can never be ascertained, probably because it really has none, but is only a pseudo-language." Flournoy, p. 199. ". . . analogous to the gibberish which children use sometimes in their games of 'pretending' to speak Chinese, Indian, or 'savage'. . ." (p. 159, modified).

sists only in the unconscious use of different impressions, some optical, some acoustic, and all very obvious.

145   (2) *The cryptomnesic image enters consciousness through mediation of the senses, as an hallucination.* Hélène Smith is the classic example of this. See the case cited above, concerning the number 18 [par. 98].

146   (3) *The image enters consciousness by motor automatism.* Hélène Smith had lost a very valuable brooch which she was anxiously looking for everywhere. Ten days later her guide Leopold told her by table movements where it was. From the information received, she found it one night in an open field, covered by sand.[130] Strictly speaking, in cryptomnesia there is no heightened performance in the true sense of the term, since the conscious memory experiences no intensification of function but only an enrichment of content. Through the automatism certain areas which were previously closed to consciousness are made accessible to it in an indirect way, but the unconscious itself is not performing any function that exceeds the capacities of the conscious mind either qualitatively or quantitatively. Cryptomnesia is therefore only an apparent instance of heightened performance, in contrast to hypermnesia, where there is an actual increase of function.[131]

147   We spoke earlier of the unconscious having a receptivity superior to that of the conscious mind, chiefly in regard to simple thought-transference experiments with numbers. As already mentioned, not only our somnambulist but a fairly large number of normal people are able to guess, from tremor movements, quite long trains of thought, provided they are not too complicated. These experiments are, so to speak, the prototype of those rarer and incomparably more astonishing cases of intuitive knowledge displayed at times by somnambulists.[132] Zschokke has shown from his own self-analysis [133] that such phenomena occur in connection not only with somnambulism but with non-somnambulists as well.

130 Ibid., p. 405.
131 For a case of this kind see Krafft-Ebing, *Text-Book of Insanity* (orig. 1879).
132 Loewenfeld (*Hypnotismus*, p. 289) writes: "The restriction of associative processes to, and the steady concentration of attention on, a definite field of representation can also lead to the development of new ideas which no effort of will in the waking state would have been able to bring to light."
133 Zschokke, *Eine Selbstschau* (1843), pp. 227ff.

148   This knowledge seems to be formed in several different ways. The first thing to be considered, as we have said, is the delicacy of unconscious perceptions; secondly, we must emphasize the importance of what proves to be the enormous suggestibility of somnambulists. The somnambulist not only incorporates every suggestive idea into himself, he actually lives himself into the suggestion, into the person of the doctor or observer, with the utter abandon characteristic of suggestible hysterics. Frau Hauffe's relation to Kerner is an excellent example of this. So it not surprising that there is in these cases a high degree of concord of associations, a fact which Richet, for instance, might have taken more account of in his experiments on thought-transference. Finally, there are cases of somnambulistic heightened performance which cannot be explained solely by the hyperaesthetic unconscious activity of the senses, or by the concord of associations, but which postulate a highly developed intellectual activity of the unconscious. To decipher the intended tremor movements requires an extraordinary delicacy of feeling, both sensitive and sensory, in order to combine the individual perceptions into a self-contained unit of thought—if indeed it is permissible at all to make an analogy between the cognitive processes in the unconscious and those of the conscious. The possibility must always be borne in mind that, in the unconscious, feelings and concepts are not so clearly separated, and may even be one. The intellectual exaltation which many somnambulists display during ecstasy, though rather uncommon, is a well-observed fact,[134] and I am inclined to regard the mystical system devised by our patient as just such an example of heightened unconscious performance that transcends her normal intelligence. We have already seen where part of that system probably comes from. Another source may be Frau Hauffe's "life-circles," depicted in Kerner's book. At any rate its outward form seems to be determined by these factors. As we have already noted, the idea of dualism derives from those fragments of conversation overheard by the patient in the dreamy state following her ecstasies.

[134] Gilles de la Tourette (quoted in Loewenfeld, p. 132) says: "We have seen somnambulistic girls, poor, uneducated, and quite stupid in the waking state, whose whole appearance altered as soon as they were put to sleep. Before they were boring, now they are lively and excited, sometimes even witty."

[4. Conclusion]

149   This exhausts my knowledge of the sources used by the patient. Where the root idea came from she was unable to say. Naturally I waded through the occult literature so far as it pertained to this subject, and discovered a wealth of parallels with our gnostic system, dating from different centuries, but scattered about in all kinds of works, most of them quite inaccessible to the patient. Moreover, at her tender age, and in her surroundings, the possibility of any such study must be ruled out of account. A brief survey of the system in the light of the patient's own explanations will show how much intelligence was expended on its construction. How high the intellectual achievement is to be rated must remain a matter of taste. At all events, considering the youth and mentality of the patient, it must be regarded as something quite out of the ordinary.

150   In conclusion, I would like to express my warmest thanks to my revered teacher, Professor Bleuler, for his friendly encouragement and the loan of books, and to my friend Dr. Ludwig von Muralt for his kindness in handing over to me the first case mentioned in this book (case of Miss E.).

ON SPIRITUALISTIC PHENOMENA[1]

697   It is impossible, within the short space of a lecture, to say any-thing fundamental about such a complicated historical and psycho-logical problem as spiritualism[1a] appears to be. One must content oneself with shedding a little light on one or the other aspect of this intricate question. This kind of approach will at least give the hearer an approximate idea of the many facets of spiritualism. Spiri-tualism, as well as being a theory (its advocates call it "scientific"), is a religious belief which, like every religious belief, forms the spiri-tual core of a religious movement. This sect believes in the actual and tangible intervention of a spiritual world in our world, and consequently makes a religious practice of communicating with the spirits. The dual nature of spiritualism gives it an advantage over other religious movements: not only does it believe in certain articles of faith that are not susceptible of proof, but it bases its belief on a body of allegedly scientific, physical phenomena which are sup-posed to be of such a nature that they cannot be explained except by the activity of spirits. Because of its dual nature—on the one side a religious sect, on the other a scientific hypothesis—spiritualism touches upon widely differing areas of life that would seem to have nothing in common.

698   Spiritualism as a sect originated in America in the year 1848. The story of its origin is a strange one.[2] Two girls of the Methodist family Fox, in Hydesville, near Rochester (New York), were fright-ened every night by sounds of knocking. At first a great scandal arose, because the neighbours suspected that the devil was up to his usual tricks. Gradually, however, communication was estab-lished with the knocking sounds when it was discovered that ques-tions were answered with a definite number of knocks. With the help of a knocking alphabet, it was learned that a man had been

---

[1] [Lecture delivered at the Bernoullianum, Basel, 5 Feb. 1905. Published serially as "Ueber spiritistische Erscheinungen" in the *Basler Nachrichten,* nos. 311–316 (12–17 Nov. 1905). Jung's original footnotes are given in full.]

[1a] [While "spiritism" (for *Spiritismus*) is the form now preferred by specialists, "spiritualism," the form in general currency, has been used in this paper and those that follow.]

[2] Detailed report in Capron, *Modern Spiritualism, Its Facts and Fanaticisms* (Boston, 1885); résumé in Aksakow, *Animismus und Spiritismus* (1894).

murdered in the Foxes' house, and his body buried in the cellar. Investigations were said to have confirmed this.

69   Thus far the report. The public performances given by the Foxes with the poltergeists were quickly followed by the founding of other sects. Tableturning, much practised earlier, was taken up again. Numerous mediums were sought and found, that is, persons in whose presence such phenomena as knocking noises occurred. The movement spread rapidly to England and the continent. In Europe, spiritualism took the form chiefly of an epidemic of table-turning. There was hardly an evening party or dance where the guests did not steal away at a late hour to question the table. This particular symptom of spiritualism was rampant everywhere. The religious sects made less headway, but they continued to grow steadily. In every big city today there is a fairly large community of practising spiritualists.

700   In America, which swarms with local religious movements, the rise of spiritualism is understandable enough. With us, its favourable reception can be explained only by the fact that the ground had been historically prepared. The beginning of the nineteenth century had brought us the Romantic Movement in literature, a symptom of a widespread, deep-seated longing for anything extraordinary and abnormal. People adored wallowing in Ossianic emotions, they went crazy over novels set in old castles and ruined cloisters. Everywhere prominence was given to the mystical, the hysterical; lectures about life after death, about sleepwalkers and visionaries, about animal magnetism and mesmerism, were the order of the day. Schopenhauer devoted a long chapter to all these things in his *Parerga und Paralipomena,* and he also spoke of them at various places in his *chef d'œuvre.*[3] Even his important concept of "sanctity" is a far-fetched, mystico-aesthetic ideal. Similar movements made themselves felt in the Catholic church, clustering round the strange figure of Johan Joseph von Görres (1776–1848). Especially significant in this respect is his four-volume work *Die christliche Mystik* (Regensburg, 1836–42). The same trends appear in his earlier book, *Emanuel Swedenborg, seine Visionen und sein Verhältnis zur Kirche* (Speyer, 1827). The Protestant public raved about the soulful poetry of Justinus Kerner and his clairvoyante, Frau Friederike Hauffe, while certain theologians gave vent to their catholicizing tendencies by excommunicating spirits. From this period, too,

---

3 [*The World as Will and Idea.*]

come a large number of remarkable psychological descriptions of abnormal people—ecstatics, somnambulists, sensitives. They were much in demand and were cultivated assiduously. A good example was Frau Hauffe herself, the clairvoyante of Prevorst, and the circle of admirers who gathered round her. Her Catholic counterpart was Katharina Emmerich, the ecstatic nun of Dulmen. Reports of similar personalities were collected together in a weighty tome by an anonymous savant, entitled "The Ecstatic Virgins of the Tyrol. Guiding Stars in the Dark Firmament of Mysticism."[4]

701   When these strange personages were investigated, the following suprasensible processes were observed:

  1. "Magnetic" phenomena.
  2. Clairvoyance and prophecy.
  3. Visions.

702   1. *Animal magnetism,* as understood at the beginning of the nineteenth century, covered a vaguely defined area of physiological and psychological phenomena which, it was thought, could all be explained as "magnetic." "Animal magnetism" had been in the air ever since the brilliant experiments of Franz Anton Mesmer. It was Mesmer who discovered the art of putting people to sleep by light passes of the hand. In some people this sleep was like the natural one, in others it was a "waking sleep"; that is, they were like sleepwalkers, only part of them was asleep, while some senses remained awake. This half-sleep was also called "magnetic sleep" or somnambulism. People in these states were wholly under the will of the magnetist, they were "magnetized" by him. Today, as we know, there is nothing wonderful about these states; they are known as hypnosis and we use the mesmeric passes as a valuable adjunct to other methods of suggestion. The significance attributed to the passes quickly led to their being grossly overestimated. People thought that some vitalistic force had been discovered; they spoke of a "magnetic fluid" that streamed from the magnetist into the patient and destroyed the diseased tissue. They also used it to explain the movements of the table in tableturning, imagining that the table was vitalized by the laying on of hands and could therefore move about like a living thing. The phenomena of the divining rod and the automatically swinging pendulum were explained in the same way. Even completely crazy phenomena of this sort were

[4] *Die Tyroler ekstatischen Jungfrauen. Leitsterne in die dunklen Gebiete der Mystik* (Regensburg, 1843).

widely reported and believed. Thus the *Neue Preussische Zeitung* reported from Barmen, in Pomerania, that a party of seven persons sat themselves round a table in a boat, and magnetized it. "In the first 20 minutes the boat drifted 50 feet downstream. Then it began to turn, with steadily increasing speed, until the rotary movement had carried it through an arc of 180 degrees in 3 minutes. Eventually, by skilful manipulation of the rudder, the boat moved forwards, and the party travelled half a mile upstream in 40 minutes, but on the return journey covered the same distance in 26 minutes. A crowd of spectators, watching the experiment from the banks of the river, received the 'table travellers' with jubilation." In very truth, a mystical motorboat! According to the report, the experiment had been suggested by a Professor Nägeli, of Freiburg im Breisgau.

703   Experiments in divination are known from the grey dawn of history. Thus Ammianus Marcellinus reports from A.D. 371 that a certain Patricius and Hilarius, living in the reign (364–78) of the Emperor Valens, had discovered by the "abominable arts of soothsaying" who would succeed to the throne. For this purpose they used a metal bowl, with the alphabet engraved round the rim. Over it, amid fearful oaths, they suspended a ring on a thread. This began to swing, and spelt out the name Theodorus. When their magic was divulged, they were arrested and put to death.

704   Ordinarily, experiments with the automatic movements of the table, the divining rod, and the pendulum are not as bizarre as the first example or as dangerous as the second. The various phenomena that may occur in tableturning have been described in a treatise by Justinus Kerner, bearing the significant title: "The Somnambulant Tables. A History and Explanation of these Phenomena"[5] (1853). They have also been described by the late Professor Thury, of Geneva, in *Les Tables parlantes au point de vue de la physique générale* (1855).

705   2. *Clairvoyance and prophecy* are further characteristics of somnambulists. Clairvoyance in time and space plays a large role in the biographies and descriptions of these cases. The literature abounds in more or less credible reports, most of which have been collected by Gurney, Myers, and Podmore in their book, *Phantasms of the Living* (1886).

706   An excellent example of clairvoyance is preserved for us in phil-

[5] *Die somnambulen Tische. Zur Geschichte und Erklärung dieser Erscheinungen.*

osophical literature and is especially interesting because it was personally commented on by Kant. In an undated letter to Charlotte von Knobloch, he wrote as follows about the spirit-seer Swedenborg: [6]

707   The following occurrence appears to me to have the greatest weight of proof, and to place the assertion respecting Swedenborg's extraordinary gift beyond all possibility of doubt.

708   In the year 1759, towards the end of September, on Saturday at four o'clock p.m., Swedenborg arrived at Gottenburg from England, when Mr. William Castel invited him to his house, together with a party of fifteen persons. About six o'clock Swedenborg went out, and returned to the company quite pale and alarmed. He said that a dangerous fire had just broken out in Stockholm, at the Södermalm (Gottenburg is about fifty German miles from Stockholm), and that it was spreading very fast. He was restless, and went out often. He said that the house of one of his friends, whom he named, was already in ashes, and that his own was in danger. At eight o'clock, after he had been out again, he joyfully exclaimed, 'Thank God! the fire is extinguished; the third door from my house.' This news occasioned great commotion throughout the whole city, but particularly amongst the company in which he was. It was announced to the Governor the same evening. On Sunday morning Swedenborg was summoned to the Governor who questioned him concerning the disaster. Swedenborg described the fire precisely, how it had begun and in what manner it had ceased, and how long it had continued. On the same day the news spread through the city, and as the Governor thought it worthy of attention, the consternation was considerably increased; because many were in trouble on account of their friends and property, which might have been involved in the disaster. On Monday evening a messenger arrived at Gottenburg, who was despatched by the Board of Trade during the time of the fire. In the letters brought by him, the fire was described precisely in the manner stated by Swedenborg. On Tuesday morning the Royal Courier arrived at the Governor's with the melancholy intelligence of the fire, of the loss which it had occasioned, and of the houses it had damaged and ruined, not in the least differing from that which Swedenborg had given at the very time when it happened; for the fire was extinguished at eight o'clock.

709   What can be brought forward against the authenticity of this occurrence (the conflagration in Stockholm)? My friend who wrote this to me has examined all, not only in Stockholm, but also, about two months ago, in Gottenburg, where he is well acquainted with the most

[6] [*Dreams of a Spirit-Seer*, trans. by E. F. Goerwitz, pp. 158ff. The unidentified text quoted by Jung gives the date 1756 for Swedenborg's experience. In the Goerwitz edn. the date 1759 is justified in Appendix III, pp. 160–61.]

respectable houses, and where he could obtain the most authentic and complete information, for as only a very short time had elapsed since 1759, most of the inhabitants are still alive who were eyewitnesses of this occurrence.

710   *Prophecy* is a phenomenon so well known from the teachings of religion that there is no need to give any examples.

711   3. *Visions* have always figured largely in miraculous tales, whether in the form of a ghostly apparition or an ecstatic vision. Science regards visions as delusions of the senses, or hallucinations. Hallucinations are very common among the insane. Let me cite an example from the literature of psychiatry:

712   A twenty-four-year-old servant girl, with an alcoholic father and a neurotic mother, suddenly begins falling into peculiar states. From time to time she falls into a state of consciousness in which she sees everything that comes into her mind vividly before her, as though it were there in reality. All the time the images keep changing with breathtaking speed and lifelikeness. The patient, who in actual life is nothing but a simple country girl, then resembles an inspired seer. Her features become transfigured, her movements flow with grace. Famous figures pass before her mind's eye. Schiller appears to her in person and plays with her. He recites his poems to her. Then she herself begins to recite, improvising in verse the things she has read, experienced, and thought. Finally she comes back to consciousness tired and exhausted, with a headache and a feeling of oppression, and with only an indistinct memory of what has happened. At other times her second consciousness has a sombre character. She sees ghostly figures prophesying disaster, processions of spirits, caravans of strange and terrifying beastlike forms, her own body being buried, etc.[7]

713   Visionary ecstasies are usually of this type. Numerous visionaries are known to us from history, among them many of the Old Testament prophets. There is the report of St. Paul's vision on the road to Damascus, followed by a blindness that ceased at the psychological moment. This blindness reminds us on the one hand of the blindness which can be produced by suggestion, and on the other hand of the blindness which occurs spontaneously with certain hysterical patients and again disappears at a suitable psychological moment. The best visions, and the ones that are psychologically the most transparent, are found in the legends of the saints, the visions being most colourful in the case of female saints experiencing

[7] Krafft-Ebing, *Lehrbuch der Psychiatrie* [Buch III, Teil III, cap. 3, Beob. 68; cf. trans. by C. G. Chaddock, *Text-book of Insanity*, p. 495, case 52].

the heavenly marriage. An outstanding visionary type was the Maid of Orleans, who was unconsciously imitated by the devout dreamer Thomas Ignaz Martin at the time of Louis XVIII.[8]

714   Swedenborg, a learned and highly intelligent man, was a visionary of unexampled fertility. His importance is attested by the fact that he had a considerable influence on Kant.[9]

715   These remarks are not meant to be conclusive, they are only intended to sketch in broad outline the state of knowledge at that time and its mystical tendency. They give some idea of the psychological premises which explain the rapid spread of American spiritualism in Europe. The tableturning epidemic of the fifties has already been mentioned. It reached a climax in the sixties and seventies. In Paris, spiritualistic séances were held at the court of Napoleon III. Famous and sometimes infamous mediums appeared —Cumberland, the Davenport brothers, Home, Slade, Miss Cook. This was the real heyday of spiritualism, for these mediums produced marvellous phenomena, quite extraordinary things which went so far beyond the bounds of credibility that a thinking person who was not himself an eyewitness could only treat them with scepticism. The impossible happened: human bodies, and parts of bodies, materialized out of thin air, bodies that had an intelligence of their own and declared themselves to be the spirits of the dead. They complied with the doubting requests of the worldlings and even submitted to experimental conditions; on vanishing from this world, they left behind pieces of their white gauzy robes, prints of their hands and feet, handwriting on the inner side of two slates sealed together, and, finally, even let themselves be photographed.

716   But the full impact of these tidings, impressive as they were, was not felt until the famous English physicist, William Crookes, in his *Quarterly Journal of Science,* presented to the world a report on the observations he had made during the past eight years, which had convinced him of the reality of the phenomena in question. Since the report is concerned with observations at which none of us was present, under conditions which it is no longer possible to check, we have no alternative but to let the observer himself inform us how these observations were mirrored in his brain. The tone

---

[8] Cf. Kerner, *Die Geschichte des Thomas Ignaz Martin, Landsmanns zu Gallardon, über Frankreich und dessen Zukunft im Jahre 1816 geschaut* (Heilbronn, 1835).

[9] Cf. Gilbert Ballet, *Swedenborg: Histoire d'un visionnaire au XVIII siècle* (Paris, 1899).

of the report at least allows us to surmise the state of his feelings at the time of writing. I shall therefore cite verbatim a passage from his investigations during the years 1870–73:[10]

CLASS VI

The Levitation of Human Beings

717   This has occurred in my presence on four occasions in darkness. The test conditions under which they took place were quite satisfactory, so far as the judgment was concerned; but ocular demonstration of such a fact is so necessary to disturb our preformed opinions as to "the naturally possible and impossible," that I will here only mention cases in which the deductions of reason were confirmed by the sense of sight.

718   On one occasion I witnessed a chair, with a lady sitting on it, rise several inches from the ground. On another occasion, to avoid the suspicion of this being in some way performed by herself, the lady knelt on the chair in such manner that its four feet were visible to us. It then rose about three inches, remained suspended for about ten seconds, and then slowly descended. At another time two children, on separate occasions, rose from the floor with their chairs, in full daylight, under (to me) most satisfactory conditions; for I was kneeling and keeping close watch upon the feet of the chair, and observing that no one might touch them.

719   The most striking cases of levitation which I have witnessed have been with Mr. Home. On three separate occasions have I seen him raised completely from the floor of the room. Once sitting in an easy chair, once kneeling on his chair, and once standing up. On each occasion I had full opportunity of watching the occurrence as it was taking place.

720   There are at least a hundred recorded instances of Mr. Home's rising from the ground, in the presence of as many separate persons, and I have heard from the lips of the three witnesses to the most striking occurrence of this kind—the Earl of Dunraven, Lord Lindsay, and Captain C. Wynne—their own most minute accounts of what took place. To reject the recorded evidence on this subject is to reject all human testimony whatever; for no fact in sacred or profane history is supported by a stronger array of proofs.

721   The accumulated testimony establishing Mr. Home's levitations is overwhelming. It is greatly to be desired that some person, whose evidence would be accepted as conclusive by the scientific world—if indeed there lives a person whose testimony *in favour* of such phenomena

10 ["Notes of an Enquiry into the Phenomena called Spiritual, during the years 1870–73," *Quarterly Journal of Science* (London), XI (n.s., IV) (1874), 85–86.]

would be taken—would seriously and patiently examine these alleged facts. Most of the eye-witnesses to these levitations are now living, and would, doubtless, be willing to give their evidence. But, in a few years, such *direct* evidence will be difficult, if not impossible, to be obtained.

722   It is obvious from the tone of this passage that Crookes was completely convinced of the reality of his observations. I refrain from further quotations because they would not tell us anything new. It is sufficient to remark that Crookes saw pretty well everything that occurred with these great mediums. It is hardly necessary to stress that if this unprecedented happening is an actual fact, the world and science have been enriched by an experience of the most tremendous importance. For a variety of reasons, it is not possible to criticize Crookes's powers of apprehension and retention during those years from the psychiatric point of view. We only know that at that time Crookes was not manifestly insane. Crookes and his observations must remain for the present an unsolved psychological enigma. The same is true of a number of other observers whose intelligence and honesty one does not wish to disparage without good reason. Of numerous other observers, noted for their prejudices, lack of criticism, and exuberant imagination, I shall say nothing: they are ruled out from the start.

723   One does not have to be particularly beset by doubts as to whether our knowledge of the world in the twentieth century has really attained the highest possible peak to feel humanly touched by this forthright testimony of an eminent scholar. But, in spite of our sympathy, we may leave out of account the question of the physical reality of such phenomena, and instead turn our attention to the psychological question: how does a thinking person, who has shown his sober-mindedness and gift for scientific observation to good advantage in other fields, come to assert that something inconceivable is a reality?

724   This psychological interest of mine has prompted me to keep track of persons who are gifted as mediums. My profession as a psychiatrist gave me ample opportunities for this, particularly in a city like Zurich. So many remarkable elements converging in so small a space can perhaps be found nowhere else in Europe. In the last few years I have investigated eight mediums, six of them women and two of them men. The total impression made by these investigations can be summed up by saying that one must approach a medium with a minimum of expectations if one does not want to be disappointed. The results are of purely psychological interest,

and no physical or physiological novelties came to light. Everything that may be considered a scientifically established fact belongs to the domain of the mental and cerebral processes and is fully explicable in terms of the laws already known to science.

725   All phenomena which the spiritualists claim as evidence of the activity of spirits are connected with the presence of certain persons, the mediums themselves. I was never able to observe happenings alleged to be "spiritual" in places or on occasions when no medium was present. Mediums are as a rule slightly abnormal mentally. Frau Rothe, for example, although she could not be declared *non compos mentis* by forensic psychiatrists, nevertheless exhibited a number of hysterical symptoms. Seven of my mediums showed slight symptoms of hysteria (which, incidentally, are extraordinarily common in other walks of life too). One medium was an American swindler whose abnormality consisted chiefly in his impudence. The other seven acted in good faith. Only one of them, a woman of middle age, was born with her gifts; she had suffered since earliest childhood from alterations of consciousness (frequent and slightly hysterical twilight states). She made a virtue of necessity, induced the change of consciousness herself by auto-suggestion, and in this state of auto-hypnosis was able to prophesy. The other mediums discovered their gift only through social contacts and then cultivated it at spiritualistic séances, which is not particularly difficult. One can, with a few skillful suggestions, teach a remarkably high percentage of people, especially women, the simple spiritualistic manipulations, table-turning for instance, and, less commonly, automatic writing.

726   The ordinary phenomena met with in mediums are table-turning, automatic writing, and speaking in a trance.

727   Table-turning consists in one or more persons laying their hands on a table that can move easily. After a time (a couple of minutes to an hour) the table begins to move, making turning or rocking movements. This phenomenon can be observed in the case of all objects that are touched. The automatically swinging pendulum and the divining rod are based on the same principle. It was, then, a very childish hypothesis to assume, as in earlier decades, that the objects touched moved of themselves, like living things. If a fairly heavy object is chosen, and one feels the arm muscles of the medium while the object is moving, the muscular tension is immediately apparent, and hence also the effort of the medium to move the object. The only remarkable thing is that the mediums assert

they feel nothing of this effort, but, on the contrary, have a definite feeling that the object is moving of its own accord, or else that their arm or hand is moved for them. This psychological phenomenon is strange only to people who know nothing of hypnosis. A hypnotized person can be told that, on waking, he will forget everything that happened under the hypnosis, but that at a certain sign he will, without knowing why, suddenly raise his right arm. Sure enough, on waking, he has forgotten everything; at the sign he raises his right arm, without knowing why—his arm "simply rose up in the air of its own accord."

728   Spontaneous phenomena can occasionally be observed in hysterics, for instance the paralysis or peculiar automatic movements of an arm. Either the patients cannot give the reasons for these sudden symptoms, or they give the wrong reasons; for instance, the symptom came from their having caught cold, or from overstrain. One has only to hypnotize the patient in order to discover the real reason and the significance of the symptom. For instance, a young girl wakes up in the morning to find that her right arm is paralysed. She rushes in terror to the doctor and tells him she doesn't know how it happened, she must obviously have overstrained herself doing the housework the day before. That is the only reason she can think of. Under hypnosis it turns out that the day before she had a violent quarrel with her parents, and that her father grabbed her by the right arm and pushed her out of the door. The paralysis of the arm is now clear; it is connected with the unconscious memory of yesterday's scene, which was not present in her waking consciousness. (The existence of "unconscious ideas" is discussed in my paper "The Reaction-time Ratio in the Association Experiment."[11])

729   It is evident from these facts that our bodies can easily execute automatic movements whose cause and origin are not known to us. And if science had not drawn our attention to it, we would not know, either, that our arms and hands are constantly making slight movements, called "intended tremors," which accompany our thoughts. If, for instance, one vividly imagines a simple geometrical figure, a triangle, say, the tremors of the outstretched hand will also describe a triangle, as can be demonstrated very easily by means of a suitable apparatus. Hence, if we sit down at the table with a lively expectation of automatic movements, the intended tremors will reflect this expectation and gradually cause the table to move.

[11] [C.W., vol. 2.]

But once we have felt the apparently automatic movement, we are immediately convinced that "the thing works." The conviction (suggestion) clouds our judgment and observation, so that we do not notice how the tremors, very slight at first, gradually build up into muscular contractions which then naturally produce stronger and stronger and still more convincing effects.

730   Now if an ordinary table, whose simple construction we know, can execute movements apparently of its own accord and behave as if it were alive, then human fantasy is quite ready to believe that the cause of the movement is some mystic fluid or even the spirits of the air. And if, as usually happens, the table composes sentences with an intelligible content out of the letters of the alphabet, then it seems proved beyond a doubt that an "alien intelligence" is at work. We know, however, that the initial, automatic tremors are in large measure dependent on our ideas. If they are capable of moving the table, they can equally well guide its movements in such a way that they construct words and sentences out of the alphabet. Nor is it necessary to visualize the sentence beforehand. The unconscious part of the psyche which controls the automatic movements very soon causes an intellectual content to flow into them.[12] As might be expected, the intellectual content is as a rule on a very low level and only in exceptional cases exceeds the intelligence of the medium. A good example of the poverty of "table-talking" is given in Allan Kardec's *Buch der Medien*.

731   "Automatic writing" follows the same principles as table-turning. The content of the writing is in no way superior to that of "table-talking." The same considerations apply to talking in a trance or ecstasy. Instead of the muscles of the arm and hand, it is the muscles of the speech apparatus that start functioning independently. The content of trance communications is naturally on the same level as the products of the other automatisms.

732   These phenomena are statistically the ones most commonly observed in mediums. Clairvoyance is much rarer. Only two of my mediums had the reputation of being clairvoyant. One of them is a well-known professional, who has already made a fool of herself in various cities in Switzerland. In order to assess her mental state as fairly as possible, I had nearly thirty sittings with her over a period of six months. The results of the investigation, so far as clairvoyance is concerned, can be put very briefly: nothing that

[12] For a detailed account of these phenomena, see my "On the Psychology and Pathology of So-Called Occult Phenomena" (C.W., vol. 1, pars. 79ff.).

quite unquestionably exceeded the normal psychological capacities was observed. On the other hand, she did in some instances display a remarkably fine gift for unconscious combination. She could combine "petites perceptions" and guesses and evaluate them in a very skilful way, mostly in a state of slight clouding of consciousness. There is nothing supernatural about this state; on the contrary, it is a well-known subject of psychological research.

733   How delicate is the capacity for unconscious apprehension could be demonstrated experimentally with my second medium. The experiments were conducted as follows. The medium sat opposite me at a small table that stood on a thick soft carpet (to assist greater mobility). Both of us laid our hands on the table. While the medium's mind was occupied by her engaging in conversation with a third person, I thought intensively of a number between 0 and 10—for instance, 3. The arrangement was that the table had to indicate the number thought of by the same number of tilts. The fact that the number was indicated correctly each time when I kept my hands on the table throughout the experiment is not remarkable. What is remarkable is that in 77 per cent of the cases the correct number was also given when I removed my hands immediately after the first tilt. If my hands did not touch the table at all, there were no correct scores. The results of numerous experiments showed that by means of intended tremors it is possible to communicate a number between 0 and 10 to another person, in such a way that though this person could not recognize the number, he could nevertheless reproduce it by automatic movements. I was able to establish to my satisfaction that the conscious mind of the medium never had any inkling of the number I had communicated. Numbers above 10 were reproduced very uncertainly, sometimes only one of the numerals being given. If I thought of the numbers in Roman instead of Arabic numerals, the results were considerably worse. The aforesaid 77 per cent correct scores applies only to experiments with Arabic numerals. From this one can conclude that my unconscious movements must have communicated a pictorial image of the numbers. The more complicated and less customary images of Roman numerals fared worse, as was also the case with numbers above 10.

734   I cannot report these experiments without recalling a curious and instructive observation I made one day when all the psychological experiments with the medium went wrong. Even the experiments with numbers failed to come off, until I finally hit on the

following expedient: In an experiment conducted along much the same lines, I told the medium that the number I was thinking of (3) was between 2 and 5. I then got the table to answer me a dozen times. The numbers it reproduced with iron consistency were 2, 4, and 5, but never 3; thus indicating, negatively but quite clearly, that the table, or rather the unconscious of the medium, was well aware of the number I was thinking of and avoided it out of mere caprice. The capriciousness of the unconscious is something the spiritualists could tell us a good deal about, only in their language it would be said that the good spirits had been supplanted by mischievous mocking spirits who had ruined the experiment.

735   The sensitive apprehension of the unconscious, shown by its capacity to translate another person's tremors into numbers, is a striking but by no means unprecedented fact. There are numerous corroborative examples in the scientific literature. But if the unconscious, as my experiments prove, is capable of registering and reproducing something without the conscious mind knowing anything about it, then the greatest caution is necessary in evaluating clairvoyant performances. Before we jump to the conclusion that thought flies through time and space detached from the brain, we should seek to discover by meticulous psychological investigation the hidden sources of the apparently supernatural knowledge.

736   On the other hand, any unprejudiced investigator will readily admit that we do not stand today on the pinnacle of all wisdom, and that nature still has infinite possibilities up her sleeve which may be revealed in happier days to come. I shall therefore confine myself to pointing out that the cases I observed of supposed clairvoyance might easily be explained in another and more intelligible way than by the assumption of mystic powers of cognition. The apparently inexplicable cases of clairvoyance I know only by hearsay, or have read of in books.

737   The same is true of that other great class of spiritualistic manifestations, the *physical* phenomena. Those I saw were reputed to be such, but in fact were not. Generally speaking, among the countless believers in miracles of our days very few will be found who have ever seen anything manifestly supernatural. And among these few there will be still fewer who do not suffer from an overheated imagination and do not replace critical observation by faith. Nevertheless, we are left with a residue of witnesses who ought not to be cavilled at. Among these I would include Crookes.

738   All human beings are bad observers of things that are unfamiliar to them. Crookes, too, is a human being. There is no universal gift for observation that could claim a high degree of certainty without special training. Human observation achieves something only when trained in a definite field. Take a sensitive observer away from his microscope and turn his attention to wind and weather, and he is more helpless than any hunter or peasant. If we plump a good physicist down in the deceptive, magical darkness of a spiritualistic séance, with hysterical mediums plying their trade with all the incredible refinement many of them have at their command, his observation will be no more acute than a layman's. Everything will then depend on the strength of his prejudice for or against. In this respect the psychic disposition of a man like Crookes would be worth investigating. If as a result of environmental influence and education, or his innate temperament, he is not disinclined to believe in miracles, he will be convinced by the apparition. But if he is disinclined from the start to believe in miracles, he will remain unconvinced in spite of the apparition, just as did many other people who witnessed similar things with the same medium.

739   Human observation and reporting are subject to disturbance by countless sources of error, many of which are still quite unknown. For instance, a whole school of experimental psychology is now studying the "psychology of evidence," that is, the problem of observation and reporting. Professor William Stern,[13] the founder of this school, has published experiments which show man's powers of observation in a bad light. And yet Stern's experiments were conducted on educated people! It seems to me that we must go on working patiently for a few more years in the direction of the Stern school before we tackle the difficult question of the reality of spiritualistic phenomena.

740   So far as the miraculous reports in the literature are concerned, we should, for all our criticism, never lose sight of the limitations of our knowledge, otherwise something embarrassingly human might happen, making us feel as foolish as the academicians felt over Chladni's meteors,[14] or the highly respected Bavarian Board

[13] [(1871–1938), professor of applied psychology, Breslau U.; at Duke U., in the U.S.A., 1934–38. See *The Freud/Jung Letters,* index, s.v., and "The Psychological Diagnosis of Evidence" (C.W., vol. 2), par. 728.]

[14] [Correctly, meteorites, which even into the 19th cent. astronomers believed of terrestrial origin. The German physicist E.F.F. Chladni (1756–1827) advocated the theory of extra-terrestrial origin.]

of Physicians over the railway.[15] Nevertheless I believe that the present state of affairs gives us reason enough to wait quietly until more impressive physical phenomena put in an appearance. If, after making allowance for conscious and unconscious falsification, self-deception, prejudice, etc., we should still find something positive behind them, then the exact sciences will surely conquer this field by experiment and verification, as has happened in every other realm of human experience. That many spiritualists brag about their "science" and "scientific knowledge" is, of course, irritating nonsense. These people are lacking not only in criticism but in the most elementary knowledge of psychology. At bottom they do not want to be taught any better, but merely to go on believing—surely the naïvest of presumptions in view of our human failings.

[15] [When the first German railway was opened, in 1835, from Nuremberg to Fürth, the Board of Physicians held that the speed of the trains would cause dizziness in travellers and onlookers and would sour the milk of cows grazing near the tracks.]

THE PSYCHOLOGICAL FOUNDATIONS
OF BELIEF IN SPIRITS [1]

570   If we look back into the past history of mankind, we find, among many other religious convictions, a universal belief in the existence of phantoms or ethereal beings who dwell in the neighbourhood of men and who exercise an invisible yet powerful influence upon them. These beings are generally supposed to be the spirits or souls of the dead. This belief is to be found among highly civilized peoples as well as among Australian aborigines, who are still living in the Stone Age. Among Western peoples, however, belief in spirits has been counteracted by the rationalism and scientific enlightenment of the last one hundred and fifty years, so that among the majority of educated people today it has been suppressed along with other metaphysical beliefs.

[1] Originally translated by H. G. Baynes from a German manuscript and published in *Proceedings of the Society for Psychical Research* (London), XXXI (1920), having been read at a general meeting of the Society on July 4, 1919. This translation was republished in *Contributions to Analytical Psychology* (London and New York, 1928). The German original was first published as "Die psychologischen Grundlagen des Geisterglaubens," in *Über die Energetik der Seele* (Psychologische Abhandlungen, II; Zurich, 1928), and was revised and expanded in *Über psychische Energetik und das Wesen der Träume* (Zurich, 1948). The latter version is here translated, but the Baynes translation has also been consulted.—EDITORS.]

571   But just as these beliefs are still alive among the masses, so too is the belief in spirits. The "haunted house" has not yet become extinct even in the most enlightened and the most intellectual cities, nor has the peasant ceased to believe in the bewitching of his cattle. On the contrary, in this age of materialism—the inevitable consequence of rationalistic enlightenment—there has been a revival of the belief in spirits, but this time on a higher level. It is not a relapse into the darkness of superstition, but an intense scientific interest, a need to direct the searchlight of truth on to the chaos of dubious facts. The names of Crookes, Myers, Wallace, Zöllner, and many other eminent men symbolize this rebirth and rehabilitation of the belief in spirits. Even if the real nature of their observations be disputed, even if they can be accused of errors and self-deception, these investigators have still earned for themselves the undying moral merit of having thrown the full weight of their authority and of their great scientific name into these endeavours to shed fresh light on the darkness, regardless of all personal fears and considerations. They shrank neither from academic prejudice nor from the derision of the public, and at the very time when the thinking of educated people was more than ever spellbound by materialistic dogmas, they drew attention to phenomena of psychic provenience that seemed to be in complete contradiction to the materialism of their age.

572   These men typify the reaction of the human mind against the materialistic view of the world. Looked at from the historical standpoint, it is not at all surprising that they used the belief in spirits as the most effective weapon against the mere truth of the senses, for belief in spirits has the same functional significance also for primitive man. His utter dependence on circumstances and environment, the manifold distresses and tribulations of his life, surrounded by hostile neighbours, dangerous beasts of prey, and often exposed to the pitiless forces of nature; his keen senses, his cupidity, his uncontrolled emotions —all these things bind him to the physical realities, so that he is in constant danger of adopting a purely materialistic attitude and becoming degenerate. His belief in spirits, or rather, his awareness of a spiritual world, pulls him again and again out of that bondage in which his senses would hold him; it forces on him the certainty of a spiritual reality whose laws he must ob-

serve as carefully and as guardedly as the laws of his physical environment. Primitive man, therefore, really lives in two worlds. Physical reality is at the same time spiritual reality. The physical world is undeniable, and for him the world of spirits has an equally real existence, not just because he thinks so, but because of his naïve awareness of things spiritual. Wherever this naïveté is lost through contact with civilization and its disastrous "enlightenment," he forfeits his dependence on spiritual law and accordingly degenerates. Even Christianity cannot save him from corruption, for a highly developed religion like Christianity demands a highly developed psyche if its beneficial effects are to be felt.

573   For the primitive, the phenomenon of spirits is direct evidence for the reality of a spiritual world. If we inquire what these spirit-phenomena mean to him, and in what they consist, we find that the most frequent phenomenon is the seeing of apparitions, or ghosts. It is generally assumed that the seeing of apparitions is far commoner among primitives than among civilized people, the inference being that this is nothing but superstition, because civilized people do not have such visions unless they are ill. It is quite certain that civilized man makes much less use of the hypothesis of spirits than the primitive, but in my view it is equally certain that psychic phenomena occur no less frequently with civilized people than they do with primitives. The only difference is that where the primitive speaks of ghosts, the European speaks of dreams and fantasies and neurotic symptoms, and attributes less importance to them than the primitive does. I am convinced that if a European had to go through the same exercises and ceremonies which the medicine-man performs in order to make the spirits visible, he would have the same experiences. He would interpret them differently, of course, and devalue them, but this would not alter the facts as such. It is well known that Europeans have very curious psychic experiences if they have to live under primitive conditions for a long time, or if they find themselves in some other unusual psychological situation.

574   One of the most important sources of the primitive belief in spirits is dreams. People very often appear as the actors in dreams, and the primitive readily believes them to be spirits or ghosts. The dream has for him an incomparably higher value

than it has for civilized man. Not only does he talk a great deal
about his dreams, he also attributes an extraordinary importance
to them, so that it often seems as though he were unable to distinguish between them and reality. To the civilized man dreams
as a rule appear valueless, though there are some people who
attach great significance to certain dreams on account of their
weird and impressive character. This peculiarity lends plausi-
bility to the view that dreams are inspirations. But inspiration
implies something that inspires, a spirit or ghost, although this
logical inference is not likely to appeal to the modern mind. A
good instance of this is the fact that the dead sometimes appear
in dreams; the primitive naïvely takes them for revenants.

575   Another source of the belief in spirits is psychogenic diseases,
nervous disorders, especially those of an hysterical character,
which are not rare among primitives. Since these illnesses stem
from psychic conflicts, mostly unconscious, it seems to the primitive that they are caused by certain persons, living or dead, who
are in some way connected with his subjective conflict. If the
person is dead, it is naturally assumed that his spirit is having
an injurious influence. As pathogenic conflicts usually go back
to childhood and are connected with memories of the parents,
we can understand why the primitive attaches special importance to the spirits of dead relatives. This accounts for the wide
incidence of ancestor-worship, which is primarily a protection
against the malice of the dead. Anyone who has had experience
of nervous illnesses knows how great is the importance of paren-
tal influences on patients. Many patients feel persecuted by their
parents long after they are dead. The psychological after-effects
of the parents are so powerful that many cultures have developed a whole system of ancestor-worship to propitiate them.[2]

576   There can be no doubt that mental illnesses play a signifi-

2 When I was on an expedition to Mount Elgon (East Africa) in 1925–26, one
of our water-bearers, a young woman who lived in a neighbouring kraal, fell
ill with what looked like a septic abortion with high fever. We were unable to
treat her from our meagre medical supplies, so her relatives immediately sent
for a *nganga*, a medicine-man. When he arrived, the medicine-man walked
round and round the hut in ever-widening circles, snuffing the air. Suddenly he
came to a halt on a track that led down from the mountain, and explained that
the sick girl was the only daughter of parents who had died young and were now
up there in the bamboo forest. Every night they came down to make their
daughter ill so that she should die and keep them company. On the instructions

111

cant part in causing belief in spirits. Among primitive peoples these illnesses, so far as is known, are mostly of a delirious, hallucinatory or catatonic nature, belonging apparently to the broad domain of schizophrenia, an illness which covers the great majority of chronically insane patients. In all ages and all over the world, insane people have been regarded as possessed by evil spirits, and this belief is supported by the patient's own hallucinations. The patients are tormented less by visions than by auditory hallucinations: they hear "voices." Very often these voices are those of relatives or of persons in some way connected with the patient's conflicts. To the naïve mind, the hallucinations naturally appear to be caused by spirits.

577 It is impossible to speak of belief in spirits without at the same time considering the belief in souls. Belief in souls is a correlate of belief in spirits. Since, according to primitive belief, a spirit is usually the ghost of one dead, it must once have been the soul of a living person. This is particularly the case wherever the belief is held that people have only one soul. But this assumption does not prevail everywhere; it is frequently supposed that people have two or more souls, one of which survives death and is immortal. In this case the spirit of the dead is only one of the several souls of the living. It is thus only a part of the total soul—a psychic fragment, so to speak.

578 Belief in souls is therefore a necessary premise for belief in spirits, at least so far as the spirits of the dead are concerned. However, primitives do not believe only in spirits of the dead. There are also elemental demons who are supposed never to have been human souls or soul-parts. This group of spirits must therefore have a different origin.

579 Before going into the psychological grounds for belief in souls I should like to take a quick glance back at the facts already mentioned. I have pointed out three main sources that put the belief in spirits on a solid foundation: the seeing of apparitions, dreams, and pathological disturbances of psychic life. The commonest and most normal of these phenomena is

of the medicine-man a "ghost-trap" was then built on the mountain path, in the form of a little hut, and a clay figure of the sick girl was placed inside it together with some food. During the night the ghosts went in there, thinking to be with their daughter. To our boundless astonishment the girl recovered within two days. Was our diagnosis wrong? The puzzle remained unsolved.

the dream, and its great significance for primitive psychology is now widely recognized. What, then, is a dream?

580   A dream is a psychic product originating in the sleeping state without conscious motivation. In a dream, consciousness is not completely extinguished; there is always a small remnant left. In most dreams, for instance, there is still some consciousness of the ego, although it is a very limited and curiously distorted ego known as the dream-ego. It is a mere fragment or shadow of the waking ego. Consciousness exists only when psychic contents are associated with the ego, and the ego is a psychic complex of a particularly solid kind. As sleep is seldom quite dreamless, we may assume that the activity of the ego-complex seldom ceases entirely; its activity is as a rule only restricted by sleep. The psychic contents associated with it in a dream confront the ego in much the same way as do the outward circumstances in real life, so that in dreams we generally find ourselves in situations such as we could not conceive when awake, but which are very like the situations we are confronted with in reality. As in our waking state, real people and things enter our field of vision, so the dream-images enter like another kind of reality into the field of consciousness of the dream-ego. We do not feel as if we were producing the dreams, it is rather as if the dreams came to us. They are not subject to our control but obey their own laws. They are obviously autonomous psychic complexes which form themselves out of their own material. We do not know the source of their motives, and we therefore say that dreams come from the unconscious. In saying this, we assume that there are independent psychic complexes which elude our conscious control and come and go according to their own laws. In our waking life, we imagine we make our own thoughts and can have them when we want them. We also think we know where they come from, and why and to what end we have them. Whenever a thought comes to us against our will, or suddenly vanishes against our will, we feel as if something exceptional or even morbid had happened. The difference between psychic activity in the waking and in the sleeping state seems, therefore, to be an important one. In the waking state the psyche is apparently under the control of the conscious will, but in the sleeping state it produces contents that are strange and incomprehensible, as though they came from another world.

581   The same is true of visions. They are like dreams, only they occur in the waking state. They enter consciousness along with conscious perceptions and are nothing other than the momentary irruption of an unconscious content. The same phenomenon also happens in mental disturbances. Quite out of the blue, apparently, against the background of noises in the environment and sound-waves coming from outside, the ear, excited from within, hears psychic contents that have nothing to do with the immediate concerns of the conscious mind.[3] Besides judgments formed by intellect and feeling from definite premises, opinions and convictions thrust themselves on the patient, apparently deriving from real perceptions but actually from unconscious factors within him. These are delusional ideas.

582   Common to all three types of phenomena is the fact that the psyche is not an indivisible unity but a divisible and more or less divided whole. Although the separate parts are connected with one another, they are relatively independent, so much so that certain parts of the psyche never become associated with the ego at all, or only very rarely. I have called these psychic fragments "autonomous complexes," and I based my theory of complexes on their existence.[4] According to this theory the ego-complex forms the centre characteristic of our psyche. But it is only one among several complexes. The others are more often than not associated with the ego-complex and in this way become conscious, but they can also exist for some time without being associated with it. An excellent and very well known example of this is the conversion of St. Paul. Although the actual moment of conversion often seems quite sudden and unexpected, we know from experience that such a fundamental upheaval always requires a long period of incubation. It is only when this preparation is complete, that is to say when the individual is ripe for conversion, that the new insight breaks through with violent emotion. Saul, as he was then called, had unconsciously been a Christian for a long time, and this would explain his fanatical hatred of the Christians, because fanaticism is always found in those who have to stifle a secret doubt. That is why converts are always the worst fanatics. The vision of Christ on the road to Damascus merely marks the moment when the

[3] There are even cases where the voices repeat the patient's thoughts aloud. But these are rather rare.   [4] Cf. "A Review of the Complex Theory," in C.W. 8.

unconscious Christ-complex associated itself with Paul's ego. The fact that Christ appeared to him objectively, in the form of a vision, is explained by the circumstance that Saul's Christianity was an unconscious complex which appeared to him in projection, as if it did not belong to him. He could not see himself as a Christian; therefore, from sheer resistance to Christ, he became blind and could only be healed again by a Christian. We know that psychogenic blindness is always an unconscious unwillingness to see, which in Saul's case corresponds with his fanatical resistance to Christianity. This resistance, as we know from the Epistles, was never entirely overcome, and occasionally it broke out in the form of fits which are erroneously explained as epileptic. The fits were a sudden return of the old Saul-complex which had been split off by his conversion just as the Christ-complex was before.

583   For reasons of intellectual morality, we should not explain Paul's conversion on metaphysical grounds, otherwise we should have to explain all similar cases that occur among our patients in the same metaphysical way. This would lead to quite absurd conclusions repugnant to reason and feeling alike.

584   Autonomous complexes appear most clearly in dreams, visions, pathological hallucinations, and delusional ideas. Because the ego is unconscious of them, they always appear first in projected form. In dreams they are represented by other people, in visions they are projected, as it were, into space, just like the voices in insanity when not ascribed to persons in the patient's environment. Ideas of persecution, as we know, are frequently associated with particular persons to whom the patient attributes the peculiarities of his own unconscious complex. He feels these persons as hostile because he is hostile to the unconscious complex, just as Saul resented the Christ-complex he could not acknowledge in himself and persecuted the Christians as its representatives. We see this constantly repeated in everyday life: people unhesitatingly project their own assumptions about others on to the persons concerned and hate or love them accordingly. Since reflection is so troublesome and difficult, they prefer to judge without restraint, not realizing that they are merely projecting and making themselves the victims of a stupid illusion. They take no account of the injustice and uncharitable-

ness of such a procedure, and above all they never consider the serious loss of personality they suffer when, from sheer negligence, they allow themselves the luxury of foisting their own mistakes or merits onto others. It is exceedingly unwise to think that other people are as stupid and inferior as one is oneself, and one should also realize the damage one does by assigning one's own good qualities to moral highwaymen with an eye to the main chance.

585   Spirits, therefore, viewed from the psychological angle, are unconscious autonomous complexes which appear as projections because they have no direct association with the ego.[5]

586   I said earlier on that belief in souls is a necessary correlate of belief in spirits. Whilst spirits are felt to be strange and as not belonging to the ego, this is not true of the soul or souls. The primitive feels the proximity or the influence of a spirit as something uncanny or dangerous, and is greatly relieved when the spirit is banished. Conversely, he feels the loss of a soul as if it were a sickness; indeed, he often attributes serious physical diseases to loss of soul. There are innumerable rites for calling the "soul-bird" back into the sick person. Children may not be struck because their souls might feel insulted and depart. Thus, for the primitive, the soul is something that seems normally to belong to him, but spirits seem to be something that normally should not be near him. He avoids places haunted by spirits, or visits them only with fear, for religious or magical purposes.

587   The plurality of souls indicates a plurality of relatively autonomous complexes that can behave like spirits. The soul-complexes seem to belong to the ego and the loss of them appears pathological. The opposite is true of spirit-complexes: their association with the ego causes illness, and their dissociation from it brings recovery. Accordingly, primitive pathology recognizes two causes of illness: loss of soul, and possession by a spirit. The two theories keep one another more or less balanced. We therefore have to postulate the existence of unconscious complexes that normally belong to the ego, and of those that

5 This should not be misconstrued as a metaphysical statement. The question of whether spirits exist *in themselves* is far from having been settled. Psychology is not concerned with things as they are "in themselves," but only with what people think about them.

normally should not become associated with it. The former are the soul-complexes, the latter the spirit-complexes.

588   This distinction, common to most primitive beliefs, corresponds exactly to my conception of the unconscious. According to my view, the unconscious falls into two parts which should be sharply distinguished from one another. One of them is the personal unconscious; it includes all those psychic contents which have been forgotten during the course of the individual's life. Traces of them are still preserved in the unconscious, even if all conscious memory of them has been lost. In addition, it contains all subliminal impressions or perceptions which have too little energy to reach consciousness. To these we must add unconscious combinations of ideas that are still too feeble and too indistinct to cross over the threshold. Finally, the personal unconscious contains all psychic contents that are incompatible with the conscious attitude. This comprises a whole group of contents, chiefly those which appear morally, aesthetically, or intellectually inadmissible and are repressed on account of their incompatibility. A man cannot always think and feel the good, the true, and the beautiful, and in trying to keep up an ideal attitude everything that does not fit in with it is automatically repressed. If, as is nearly always the case in a differentiated person, one function, for instance thinking, is especially developed and dominates consciousness, then feeling is thrust into the background and largely falls into the unconscious.

589   The other part of the unconscious is what I call the impersonal or collective unconscious. As the name indicates, its contents are not personal but collective; that is, they do not belong to one individual alone but to a whole group of individuals, and generally to a whole nation, or even to the whole of mankind. These contents are not acquired during the individual's lifetime but are products of innate forms and instincts. Although the child possesses no inborn ideas, it nevertheless has a highly developed brain which functions in a quite definite way. This brain is inherited from its ancestors; it is the deposit of the psychic functioning of the whole human race. The child therefore brings with it an organ ready to function in the same way as it has functioned throughout human history. In the brain the instincts are preformed, and so are the primordial images which have always been the basis of man's thinking—the whole treas-

ure-house of mythological motifs.[6] It is, of course, not easy to prove the existence of the collective unconscious in a normal person, but occasionally mythological ideas are represented in his dreams. These contents can be seen most clearly in cases of mental derangement, especially in schizophrenia, where mythological images often pour out in astonishing variety. Insane people frequently produce combinations of ideas and symbols that could never be accounted for by experiences in their individual lives, but only by the history of the human mind. It is an instance of primitive, mythological thinking, which reproduces its own primordial images, and is not a reproduction of conscious experiences.[7]

590   The personal unconscious, then, contains complexes that belong to the individual and form an intrinsic part of his psychic life. When any complex which ought to be associated with the ego becomes unconscious, either by being repressed or by sinking below the threshold, the individual experiences a sense of loss. Conversely, when a lost complex is made conscious again, for instance through psychotherapeutic treatment, he experiences an increase of power.[8] Many neuroses are cured in this way. But when, on the other hand, a complex of the collective unconscious becomes associated with the ego, i.e., becomes conscious, it is felt as strange, uncanny, and at the same time fascinating. At all events the conscious mind falls under its spell, either feeling it as something pathological, or else being alienated by it from normal life. The association of a collective content with the ego always produces a state of alienation, because something is added to the individual's consciousness which ought really to remain unconscious, that is, separated from the ego. If the content can be removed from consciousness again, the patient will feel relieved and more normal. The irruption

[6] By this I do not mean the existing form of the motif but its preconscious, invisible "ground plan." This might be compared to the crystal lattice which is preformed in the crystalline solution. It should not be confused with the variously structured axial system of the individual crystal.

[7] Cf. my *Symbols of Transformation;* also Spielrein, "Über den psychologischen Inhalt eines Falles von Schizophrenie"; Nelken, "Analytische Beobachtungen über Phantasien eines Schizophrenen"; C. A. Meier, "Spontanmanifestationen des kollektiven Unbewussten."

[8] This is not always a pleasant feeling, for the patient was quite content to lose the complex so long as he did not feel the disagreeable consequences of the loss.

of these alien contents is a characteristic symptom marking the onset of many mental illnesses. The patients are seized by weird and monstrous thoughts, the whole world seems changed, people have horrible, distorted faces, and so on.[9]

591   While the contents of the personal unconscious are felt as belonging to one's own psyche, the contents of the collective unconscious seem alien, as if they came from outside. The reintegration of a personal complex has the effect of release and often of healing, whereas the invasion of a complex from the collective unconscious is a very disagreeable and even dangerous phenomenon. The parallel with the primitive belief in souls and spirits is obvious: souls correspond to the autonomous complexes of the personal unconscious, and spirits to those of the collective unconscious. We, from the scientific standpoint, prosaically call the awful beings that dwell in the shadows of the primeval forests "psychic complexes." Yet if we consider the extraordinary role played by the belief in souls and spirits in the history of mankind, we cannot be content with merely establishing the existence of such complexes, but must go rather more deeply into their nature.

592   These complexes can easily be demonstrated by means of the association experiment.[10] The procedure is simple. The experimenter calls out a word to the test-person, and the test-person reacts as quickly as possible with the first word that comes into his mind. The reaction time is measured by a stopwatch. One would expect all simple words to be answered with roughly the same speed, and that only "difficult" words would be followed by a prolonged reaction time. But actually this is not so. There are unexpectedly prolonged reaction times after very simple words, whereas difficult words may be answered quite quickly. Closer investigation shows that prolonged reaction times generally occur when the stimulus-word hits a content with a strong feeling-tone. Besides the prolonged reaction-time there are other

9 Those who are familiar with this material will object that my description is one-sided, because they know that the archetype, the autonomous collective content, does not have only the negative aspect described here. I have merely restricted myself to the common symptomatology that can be found in every text-book of psychiatry, and to the equally common defensive attitude towards anything extraordinary. Naturally the archetype also has a positive numinosity which I have repeatedly mentioned elsewhere.

10 Cf. my *Studies in Word Association*.

characteristic disturbances that cannot be discussed in detail here. The feeling-toned contents generally have to do with things which the test-person would like to keep secret—painful things which he has repressed, some of them being unknown even to the test-person himself. When a stimulus-word hits such a complex, no answer occurs to him at all, or else so many things crowd into his mind that he does not know what answer to give, or he mechanically repeats the stimulus-word, or he gives an answer and then immediately substitutes another, and so forth. When, after completing the experiment, the test-person is asked what answers he gave to the individual words, we find that ordinary reactions are remembered quite well, while words connected with a complex are usually forgotten.

593   These peculiarities plainly reveal the qualities of the autonomous complex. It creates a disturbance in the readiness to react, either inhibiting the answer or causing an undue delay, or it produces an unsuitable reaction, and afterwards often suppresses the memory of the answer. It interferes with the conscious will and disturbs its intentions. That is why we call it autonomous. If we subject a neurotic or insane person to this experiment, we find that the complexes which disturb the reactions are at the same time essential components of the psychic disturbance. They cause not only the disturbances of reaction but also the symptoms. I have seen cases where certain stimulus-words were followed by strange and apparently nonsensical answers, by words that came out of the test-person's mouth quite unexpectedly, as though a strange being had spoken through him. These words belonged to the autonomous complex. When excited by an external stimulus, complexes can produce sudden confusions, or violent affects, depressions, anxiety-states, etc., or they may express themselves in hallucinations. In short, they behave in such a way that the primitive theory of spirits strikes one as being an uncommonly apt formulation for them.

594   We may carry this parallel further. Certain complexes arise on account of painful or distressing experiences in a person's life, experiences of an emotional nature which leave lasting psychic wounds behind them. A bad experience of this sort often crushes valuable qualities in an individual. All these produce unconscious complexes of a personal nature. A primitive would rightly speak of a loss of soul, because certain portions of the

psyche have indeed disappeared. A great many autonomous complexes arise in this way. But there are others that come from quite a different source. While the first source is easily understood, since it concerns the outward life everyone can see, this other source is obscure and difficult to understand because it has to do with perceptions or impressions of the collective unconscious. Usually the individual tries to rationalize these inner perceptions in terms of external causes, but that does not get at the root of the matter. At bottom they are irrational contents of which the individual had never been conscious before, and which he therefore vainly seeks to discover somewhere outside him. The primitive expresses this very aptly when he says that some spirit is interfering with him. So far as I can judge, these experiences occur either when something so devastating happens to the individual that his whole previous attitude to life breaks down, or when for some reason the contents of the collective unconscious accumulate so much energy that they start influencing the conscious mind. In my view this happens when the life of a large social group or of a nation undergoes a profound change of a political, social, or religious nature. Such a change always involves an alteration of the psychological attitude. Incisive changes in history are generally attributed exclusively to external causes. It seems to me, however, that external circumstances often serve merely as occasions for a new attitude to life and the world, long prepared in the unconscious, to become manifest. Social, political, and religious conditions affect the collective unconscious in the sense that all those factors which are suppressed by the prevailing views or attitudes in the life of a society gradually accumulate in the collective unconscious and activate its contents. Certain individuals gifted with particularly strong intuition then become aware of the changes going on in it and translate these changes into communicable ideas. The new ideas spread rapidly because parallel changes have been taking place in the unconscious of other people. There is a general readiness to accept the new ideas, although on the other hand they often meet with violent resistance. New ideas are not just the enemies of the old; they also appear as a rule in an extremely unacceptable form.

595   Whenever contents of the collective unconscious become activated, they have a disturbing effect on the conscious mind,

and confusion ensues. If the activation is due to the collapse of the individual's hopes and expectations, there is a danger that the collective unconscious may take the place of reality. This state would be pathological. If, on the other hand, the activation is the result of psychological processes in the unconscious of the people, the individual may feel threatened or at any rate disoriented, but the resultant state is not pathological, at least so far as the individual is concerned. Nevertheless, the mental state of the people as a whole might well be compared to a psychosis. If the translation of the unconscious into a communicable language proves successful, it has a redeeming effect. The driving forces locked up in the unconscious are canalized into consciousness and form a new source of power, which may, however, unleash a dangerous enthusiasm.[11]

596   Spirits are not under all circumstances dangerous and harmful. They can, when translated into ideas, also have beneficial effects. A well-known example of this transformation of a content of the collective unconscious into communicable language is the miracle of Pentecost. From the point of view of the onlookers, the apostles were in a state of ecstatic intoxication ("These men are full of new wine": Acts 2 : 13). But it was just when they were in this state that they communicated the new teaching which gave expression to the unconscious expectations of the people and spread with astonishing rapidity through the whole Roman Empire.

597   Spirits are complexes of the collective unconscious which appear when the individual loses his adaptation to reality, or which seek to replace the inadequate attitude of a whole people by a new one. They are therefore either pathological fantasies or new but as yet unknown ideas.

598   The psychogenesis of the spirits of the dead seems to me to be more or less as follows. When a person dies, the feelings and emotions that bound his relatives to him lose their application to reality and sink into the unconscious, where they activate a collective content that has a deleterious effect on consciousness. The Bataks and many other primitives therefore say that when a man dies his character deteriorates, so that he is always trying to harm the living in some way. This view is obviously based on

[11] This account of the genesis of a collective psyche was written in the spring of 1919. Events since 1933 have amply confirmed it.

the experience that a persistent attachment to the dead makes life seem less worth living, and may even be the cause of psychic illnesses. The harmful effect shows itself in the form of loss of libido, depression, and physical debility. There are also universal reports of these post-mortem phenomena in the form of ghosts and hauntings. They are based in the main on psychic facts which cannot be dismissed out of hand. Very often the fear of superstition—which, strangely enough, is the concomitant of universal enlightenment—is responsible for the hasty suppression of extremely interesting factual reports which are thus lost to science. I have not only found many reports of this kind among my patients, but have also observed a few things myself. But my material is too slender for me to base any verifiable hypothesis on it. Nevertheless, I myself am convinced that ghosts and suchlike have to do with psychic facts of which our academic wisdom refuses to take cognizance, although they appear clearly enough in our dreams.

*

599   In this essay I have sketched out a psychological interpretation of the problem of spirits from the standpoint of our present knowledge of unconscious processes. I have confined myself wholly to the psychological side of the problem, and purposely avoided the question of whether spirits exist in themselves and can give evidence of their existence through material effects. I avoid this question not because I regard it as futile from the start, but because I am not in a position to adduce experiences that would prove it one way or the other. I think the reader will be as conscious as I am that it is extraordinarily difficult to find reliable evidence for the independent existence of spirits, since the usual spiritualistic communications are as a rule nothing but very ordinary products of the personal unconscious.[12] There are, nevertheless, a few exceptions worth mentioning. I would like to call attention to a remarkable case Stewart E. White has described in a number of books. Here the communications have a much profounder content than usual. For instance, a great many archetypal ideas were produced, among them the archetype of the self, so that one might almost think there had been borrowings from my writings. If we discount the possibility

12 [The rest of this paragraph was added in the 1948 Swiss edition.—EDITORS.]

of conscious plagiarism, I should say that cryptomnesic reproduction is very unlikely. It appears to be a case of genuine,
spontaneous production of a collective archetype. This is not in
itself anything extraordinary, since the archetype of the self is
met with everywhere in mythology as well as in the products of
individual fantasy. The spontaneous irruption of collective
contents whose existence in the unconscious has long been
known to psychology is part of the general tendency of medium-
istic communications to filter the contents of the unconscious
through to consciousness. I have studied a wide range of spiritualistic literature precisely for these tendencies and have come
to the conclusion that in spiritualism we have a spontaneous
attempt of the unconscious to become conscious in a collective
form. The psychotherapeutic endeavours of the so-called spirits
are aimed at the living either directly, or indirectly through
the deceased person, in order to make them more conscious.
Spiritualism as a collective phenomenon thus pursues the
same goals as medical psychology, and in so doing produces, as
in this case, the same basic ideas and images—styling themselves
the "teachings of the spirits"—which are characteristic of the
nature of the collective unconscious. Such things, however
baffling they may be, prove nothing either for or against the
hypothesis of spirits. But it is a very different matter when we
come to proven cases of identity. I shall not commit the fashionable stupidity of regarding everything I cannot explain as a
fraud. There are probably very few proofs of this kind which
could stand up to the test of cryptomnesia and, above all, of
extra-sensory perception. Science cannot afford the luxury of
naïveté in these matters. Nevertheless, I would recommend anyone who is interested in the psychology of the unconscious to
read the books of Stewart White.[13] The most interesting to my
mind is *The Unobstructed Universe* (1940). *The Road I Know*
(1942) is also remarkable in that it serves as an admirable introduction to the method of "active imagination" which I have been
using for more than thirty years in the treatment of neurosis, as
a means to bringing unconscious contents to consciousness.[14] In

[13] I am indebted to Dr. Fritz Künkel, of Los Angeles, for drawing my attention to
this author.

[14] Cf. C.W. 8, "The Transcendent Function," pars. 166ff., and *Two Essays*, pars.
343ff. [Also *Mysterium Coniunctionis*, pars. 706, 752ff.]

all these books you still find the primitive equation: spirit-land = dreamland (the unconscious).

600   These parapsychic phenomena seem to be connected as a rule with the presence of a medium. They are, so far as my experience goes, the exteriorized effects of unconscious complexes. I for one am certainly convinced that they are exteriorizations. I have repeatedly observed the telepathic effects of unconscious complexes, and also a number of parapsychic phenomena. But in all this I see no proof whatever of the existence of real spirits, and until such proof is forthcoming I must regard this whole territory as an appendix of psychology.[15] I think science has to impose this restriction on itself. Yet one should never forget that science is simply a matter of intellect, and that the intellect is only one among several fundamental psychic functions and therefore does not suffice to give a complete picture of the world. For this another function—feeling—is needed too. Feeling often arrives at convictions that are different from those of the intellect, and we cannot always prove that the convictions of feeling are necessarily inferior. We also have subliminal perceptions of the unconscious which are not at the disposal of the intellect and are therefore missing in a purely intellectual picture of the world. So we have every reason to grant our intellect only a limited validity. But when we work with the intellect, we must proceed scientifically and adhere to empirical principles until irrefutable evidence against their validity is forthcoming.

15 After collecting psychological experiences from many people and many countries for fifty years, I no longer feel as certain as I did in 1919, when I wrote this sentence. To put it bluntly, I doubt whether an exclusively psychological approach can do justice to the phenomena in question. Not only the findings of parapsychology, but my own theoretical reflections, outlined in "On the Nature of the Psyche," have led me to certain postulates which touch on the realm of nuclear physics and the conception of the space-time continuum. This opens up the whole question of the transpsychic reality immediately underlying the psyche.

THE SOUL AND DEATH [1]

796   I have often been asked what I believe about death, that un-
problematical ending of individual existence. Death is known
to us simply as the end. It is the period, often placed before the
close of the sentence and followed only by memories or after-
effects in others. For the person concerned, however, the sand
has run out of the glass; the rolling stone has come to rest.
When death confronts us, life always seems like a downward
flow or like a clock that has been wound up and whose eventual
"running down" is taken for granted. We are never more convinced of this "running down" than when a human life comes
to its end before our eyes, and the question of the meaning and
worth of life never becomes more urgent or more agonizing
than when we see the final breath leave a body which a moment
before was living. How different does the meaning of life seem
to us when we see a young person striving for distant goals and
shaping the future, and compare this with an incurable invalid,
or with an old man who is sinking reluctantly and impotently

[1] [Originally published as "Seele und Tod," *Europäische Revue* (Berlin), X
(April 1934) and republished in *Wirklichkeit der Seele* (Psychologische Abhandlungen, IV; Zurich, 1934). A shortened version appeared as "Von der Psychologie
des Sterbens," *Münchner Neueste Nachrichten*, No. 269 (Oct. 2, 1935). The
present version is a slight revision of a translation by Eugene H. Henley in
Spring (Analytical Psychology Club, New York), 1945, to whom grateful acknowl-
edgment is made.—EDITORS.]

into the grave! Youth—we should like to think—has purpose, future, meaning, and value, whereas the coming to an end is only a meaningless cessation. If a young man is afraid of the world, of life and the future, then everyone finds it regrettable, senseless, neurotic; he is considered a cowardly shirker. But when an ageing person secretly shudders and is even mortally afraid at the thought that his reasonable expectation of life now amounts to only so and so many years, then we are painfully reminded of certain feelings within our own breast; we look away and turn the conversation to some other topic. The optimism with which we judge the young man fails us here. Naturally we have a stock of suitable banalities about life which we occasionally hand out to the other fellow, such as "everyone must die sometime," "you can't live forever," etc. But when one is alone and it is night and so dark and still that one hears nothing and sees nothing but the thoughts which add and subtract the years, and the long row of those disagreeable facts which remorselessly indicate how far the hand of the clock has moved forward, and the slow, irresistible approach of the wall of darkness which will eventually engulf everything I love, possess, wish for, hope for, and strive for, then all our profundities about life slink off to some undiscoverable hiding-place, and fear envelops the sleepless one like a smothering blanket.

797   Many young people have at bottom a panic fear of life (though at the same time they intensely desire it), and an even greater number of the ageing have the same fear of death. Indeed, I have known those people who most feared life when they were young to suffer later just as much from the fear of death. When they are young one says they have infantile resistances against the normal demands of life; one should really say the same thing when they are old, for they are likewise afraid of one of life's normal demands. We are so convinced that death is simply the end of a process that it does not ordinarily occur to us to conceive of death as a goal and a fulfilment, as we do without hesitation the aims and purposes of youthful life in its ascendance.

798   Life is an energy-process. Like every energy-process, it is in principle irreversible and is therefore directed towards a goal. That goal is a state of rest. In the long run everything that

happens is, as it were, no more than the initial disturbance of a perpetual state of rest which forever attempts to re-establish itself. Life is teleology *par excellence;* it is the intrinsic striving towards a goal, and the living organism is a system of directed aims which seek to fulfil themselves. The end of every process is its goal. All energy-flow is like a runner who strives with the greatest effort and the utmost expenditure of strength to reach his goal. Youthful longing for the world and for life, for the attainment of high hopes and distant goals, is life's obvious teleological urge which at once changes into fear of life, neurotic resistances, depressions, and phobias if at some point it remains caught in the past, or shrinks from risks without which the unseen goal cannot be attained. With the attainment of maturity and at the zenith of biological existence, life's drive towards a goal in no wise halts. With the same intensity and irresistibility with which it strove upward before middle age, life now descends; for the goal no longer lies on the summit, but in the valley where the ascent began. The curve of life is like the parabola of a projectile which, disturbed from its initial state of rest, rises and then returns to a state of repose.

799   The psychological curve of life, however, refuses to conform to this law of nature. Sometimes the lack of accord begins early in the ascent. The projectile ascends biologically, but psychologically it lags behind. We straggle behind our years, hugging our childhood as if we could not tear ourselves away. We stop the hands of the clock and imagine that time will stand still. When after some delay we finally reach the summit, there again, psychologically, we settle down to rest, and although we can see ourselves sliding down the other side, we cling, if only with longing backward glances, to the peak once attained. Just as, earlier, fear was a deterrent to life, so now it stands in the way of death. We may even admit that fear of life held us back on the upward slope, but just because of this delay we claim all the more right to hold fast to the summit we have now reached. Though it may be obvious that in spite of all our resistances (now so deeply regretted) life has reasserted itself, yet we pay no attention and keep on trying to make it stand still. Our psychology then loses its natural basis. Consciousness stays up in the air, while the curve of the parabola sinks downward with ever-increasing speed.

800   Natural life is the nourishing soil of the soul. Anyone who fails to go along with life remains suspended, stiff and rigid in midair. That is why so many people get wooden in old age; they look back and cling to the past with a secret fear of death in their hearts. They withdraw from the life-process, at least psychologically, and consequently remain fixed like nostalgic pillars of salt, with vivid recollections of youth but no living relation to the present. From the middle of life onward, only he remains vitally alive who is ready to *die with life*. For in the secret hour of life's midday the parabola is reversed, death is born. The second half of life does not signify ascent, unfolding, increase, exuberance, but death, since the end is its goal. The negation of life's fulfilment is synonymous with the refusal to accept its ending. Both mean not wanting to live, and not wanting to live is identical with not wanting to die. Waxing and waning make one curve.

801   Whenever possible our consciousness refuses to accommodate itself to this undeniable truth. Ordinarily we cling to our past and remain stuck in the illusion of youthfulness. Being old is highly unpopular. Nobody seems to consider that not being able to grow old is just as absurd as not being able to outgrow child's-size shoes. A still infantile man of thirty is surely to be deplored, but a youthful septuagenarian—isn't that delightful? And yet both are perverse, lacking in style, psychological monstrosities. A young man who does not fight and conquer has missed the best part of his youth, and an old man who does not know how to listen to the secrets of the brooks, as they tumble down from the peaks to the valleys, makes no sense; he is a spiritual mummy who is nothing but a rigid relic of the past. He stands apart from life, mechanically repeating himself to the last triviality.

802   Our relative longevity, substantiated by present-day statistics, is a product of civilization. It is quite exceptional for primitive people to reach old age. For instance, when I visited the primitive tribes of East Africa, I saw very few men with white hair who might have been over sixty. But they were really old, they seemed to have always been old, so fully had they assimilated their age. They were exactly what they were in every respect. We are forever only more or less than we actually are. It is as if our consciousness had somehow slipped from its natural

foundations and no longer knew how to get along on nature's timing. It seems as though we were suffering from a hybris of consciousness which fools us into believing that one's time of life is a mere illusion which can be altered according to one's desire. (One asks oneself where our consciousness gets its ability to be so contrary to nature and what such arbitrariness might signify.)

803   Like a projectile flying to its goal, life ends in death. Even its ascent and its zenith are only steps and means to this goal. This paradoxical formula is no more than a logical deduction from the fact that life strives towards a goal and is determined by an aim. I do not believe that I am guilty here of playing with syllogisms. We grant goal and purpose to the ascent of life, why not to the descent? The birth of a human being is pregnant with meaning, why not death? For twenty years and more the growing man is being prepared for the complete unfolding of his individual nature, why should not the older man prepare himself twenty years and more for his death? Of course, with the zenith one has obviously reached something, one is it and has it. But what is attained with death?

804   At this point, just when it might be expected, I do not want suddenly to pull a belief out of my pocket and invite my reader to do what nobody can do—that is, believe something. I must confess that I myself could never do it either. Therefore I shall certainly not assert now that one must believe death to be a second birth leading to survival beyond the grave. But I can at least mention that the *consensus gentium* has decided views about death, unmistakably expressed in all the great religions of the world. One might even say that the majority of these religions are complicated systems of preparation for death, so much so that life, in agreement with my paradoxical formula, actually has no significance except as a preparation for the ultimate goal of death. In both the greatest living religions, Christianity and Buddhism, the meaning of existence is consummated in its end.

805   Since the Age of Enlightenment a point of view has developed concerning the nature of religion which, although it is a typically rationalistic misconception, deserves mention because it is so widely disseminated. According to this view, all religions are something like philosophical systems, and like them are

concocted out of the head. At some time someone is supposed to have invented a God and sundry dogmas and to have led humanity around by the nose with this "wish-fulfilling" fantasy. But this opinion is contradicted by the psychological fact that the head is a particularly inadequate organ when it comes to thinking up religious symbols. They do not come from the head at all, but from some other place, perhaps the heart; certainly from a deep psychic level very little resembling consciousness, which is always only the top layer. That is why religious symbols have a distinctly "revelatory" character; they are usually spontaneous products of unconscious psychic activity. They are anything rather than thought up; on the contrary, in the course of the millennia, they have developed, plant-like, as natural manifestations of the human psyche. Even today we can see in individuals the spontaneous genesis of genuine and valid religious symbols, springing from the unconscious like flowers of a strange species, while consciousness stands aside perplexed, not knowing what to make of such creations. It can be ascertained without too much difficulty that in form and content these individual symbols arise from the same unconscious mind or "spirit" (or whatever it may be called) as the great religions of mankind. At all events experience shows that religions are in no sense conscious constructions, but that they arise from the natural life of the unconscious psyche and somehow give adequate expression to it. This explains their universal distribution and their enormous influence on humanity throughout history, which would be incomprehensible if religious symbols were not at the very least truths of man's psychological nature.

806 I know that very many people have difficulties with the word "psychological." To put these critics at ease, I should like to add that no one knows what "psyche" is, and one knows just as little how far into nature "psyche" extends. A psychological truth is therefore just as good and respectable a thing as a physical truth, which limits itself to matter as the former does to the psyche.

807 The *consensus gentium* that expresses itself through the religions is, as we saw, in sympathy with my paradoxical formula. Hence it would seem to be more in accord with the collective psyche of humanity to regard death as the fulfilment of life's meaning and as its goal in the truest sense, instead of a mere

meaningless cessation. Anyone who cherishes a rationalistic opinion on this score has isolated himself psychologically and stands opposed to his own basic human nature.

808   This last sentence contains a fundamental truth about all neuroses, for nervous disorders consist primarily in an alienation from one's instincts, a splitting off of consciousness from certain basic facts of the psyche. Hence rationalistic opinions come unexpectedly close to neurotic symptoms. Like these, they consist of distorted thinking, which takes the place of psychologically correct thinking. The latter kind of thinking always retains its connection with the heart, with the depths of the psyche, the tap-root. For, enlightenment or no enlightenment, consciousness or no consciousness, nature prepares itself for death. If we could observe and register the thoughts of a young person when he has time and leisure for day-dreaming, we would discover that, aside from a few memory-images, his fantasies are mainly concerned with the future. As a matter of fact, most fantasies consist of anticipations. They are for the most part preparatory acts, or even psychic exercises for dealing with certain future realities. If we could make the same experiment with an ageing person—without his knowledge, of course— we would naturally find, owing to his tendency to look backwards, a greater number of memory-images than with a younger person, but we would also find a surprisingly large number of anticipations, including those of death. Thoughts of death pile up to an astonishing degree as the years increase. Willynilly, the ageing person prepares himself for death. That is why I think that nature herself is already preparing for the end. Objectively it is a matter of indifference what the individual consciousness may think about it. But subjectively it makes an enormous difference whether consciousness keeps in step with the psyche or whether it clings to opinions of which the heart knows nothing. It is just as neurotic in old age not to focus upon the goal of death as it is in youth to repress fantasies which have to do with the future.

809   In my rather long psychological experience I have observed a great many people whose unconscious psychic activity I was able to follow into the immediate presence of death. As a rule the approaching end was indicated by those symbols which, in normal life also, proclaim changes of psychological condition—

rebirth symbols such as changes of locality, journeys, and the like. I have frequently been able to trace back for over a year, in a dream-series, the indications of approaching death, even in cases where such thoughts were not prompted by the outward situation. Dying, therefore, has its onset long before actual death. Moreover, this often shows itself in peculiar changes of personality which may precede death by quite a long time. On the whole, I was astonished to see how little ado the unconscious psyche makes of death. It would seem as though death were something relatively unimportant, or perhaps our psyche does not bother about what happens to the individual. But it seems that the unconscious is all the more interested in *how* one dies; that is, whether the attitude of consciousness is adjusted to dying or not. For example, I once had to treat a woman of sixty-two. She was still hearty, and moderately intelligent. It was not for want of brains that she was unable to understand her dreams. It was unfortunately only too clear that she did not *want* to understand them. Her dreams were very plain, but also very disagreeable. She had got it fixed in her head that she was a faultless mother to her children, but the children did not share this view at all, and the dreams too displayed a conviction very much to the contrary. I was obliged to break off the treatment after some weeks of fruitless effort because I had to leave for military service (it was during the war). In the meantime the patient was smitten with an incurable disease, leading after a few months to a moribund condition which might bring about the end at any moment. Most of the time she was in a sort of delirious or somnambulistic state, and in this curious mental condition she spontaneously resumed the analytical work. She spoke of her dreams again and acknowledged to herself everything that she had previously denied to me with the greatest vehemence, and a lot more besides. This self-analytic work continued daily for several hours, for about six weeks. At the end of this period she had calmed herself, just like a patient during normal treatment, and then she died.

810   From this and numerous other experiences of the kind I must conclude that our psyche is at least not indifferent to the dying of the individual. The urge, so often seen in those who are dying, to set to rights whatever is still wrong might point in the same direction.

811   How these experiences are ultimately to be interpreted is a problem that exceeds the competence of an empirical science and goes beyond our intellectual capacities, for in order to reach a final conclusion one must necessarily have had the actual experience of death. This event unfortunately puts the observer in a position that makes it impossible for him to give an objective account of his experiences and of the conclusions resulting therefrom.

812   Consciousness moves within narrow confines, within the brief span of time between its beginning and its end, and short-ened by about a third by periods of sleep. The life of the body lasts somewhat longer; it always begins earlier and, very often, it ceases later than consciousness. Beginning and end are un-avoidable aspects of all processes. Yet on closer examination it is extremely difficult to see where one process ends and another begins, since events and processes, beginnings and endings, merge into each other and form, strictly speaking, an indivisible continuum. We divide the processes from one another for the sake of discrimination and understanding, knowing full well that at bottom every division is arbitrary and conventional. This procedure in no way infringes the continuum of the world process, for "beginning" and "end" are primarily necessities of conscious cognition. We may establish with reasonable cer-tainty that an individual consciousness as it relates to ourselves has come to an end. But whether this means that the continuity of the psychic process is also interrupted remains doubtful, since the psyche's attachment to the brain can be affirmed with far less certitude today than it could fifty years ago. Psychology must first digest certain parapsychological facts, which it has hardly begun to do as yet.

813   The unconscious psyche appears to possess qualities which throw a most peculiar light on its relation to space and time. I am thinking of those spatial and temporal telepathic phe-nomena which, as we know, are much easier to ignore than to explain. In this regard science, with a few praiseworthy excep-tions, has so far taken the easier path of ignoring them. I must confess, however, that the so-called telepathic faculties of the psyche have caused me many a headache, for the catchword "telepathy" is very far from explaining anything. The limita-tion of consciousness in space and time is such an overwhelming

reality that every occasion when this fundamental truth is broken through must rank as an event of the highest theoretical significance, for it would prove that the space-time barrier can be annulled. The annulling factor would then be the psyche, since space-time would attach to it at most as a relative and conditioned quality. Under certain conditions it could even break through the barriers of space and time precisely because of a quality essential to it, that is, its relatively trans-spatial and trans-temporal nature. This possible transcendence of space-time, for which it seems to me there is a good deal of evidence, is of such incalculable import that it should spur the spirit of research to the greatest effort. Our present development of consciousness is, however, so backward that in general we still lack the scientific and intellectual equipment for adequately evaluating the facts of telepathy so far as they have bearing on the nature of the psyche. I have referred to this group of phenomena merely in order to point out that the psyche's attachment to the brain, i.e., its space-time limitation, is no longer as self-evident and incontrovertible as we have hitherto been led to believe.

814   Anyone who has the least knowledge of the parapsychological material which already exists and has been thoroughly verified will know that so-called telepathic phenomena are undeniable facts. An objective and critical survey of the available data would establish that perceptions occur as if in part there were no space, in part no time. Naturally, one cannot draw from this the metaphysical conclusion that in the world of things as they are "in themselves" there is neither space nor time, and that the space-time category is therefore a web into which the human mind has woven itself as into a nebulous illusion. Space and time are not only the most immediate certainties for us, they are also obvious empirically, since everything observable happens as though it occurred in space and time. In the face of this overwhelming certainty it is understandable that reason should have the greatest difficulty in granting validity to the peculiar nature of telepathic phenomena. But anyone who does justice to the facts cannot but admit that their apparent space-timelessness is their most essential quality. In the last analysis, our naïve perception and immediate certainty are, strictly speaking, no more than evidence of a psychological *a priori* form of percep-

tion which simply rules out any other form. The fact that we are totally unable to imagine a form of existence without space and time by no means proves that such an existence is in itself impossible. And therefore, just as we cannot draw, from an appearance of space-timelessness, any absolute conclusion about a space-timeless form of existence, so we are not entitled to conclude from the apparent space-time quality of our perception that there is no form of existence *without* space and time. It is not only permissible to doubt the absolute validity of space-time perception; it is, in view of the available facts, even imperative to do so. The hypothetical possibility that the psyche touches on a form of existence outside space and time presents a scientific question-mark that merits serious consideration for a long time to come. The ideas and doubts of theoretical physicists in our own day should prompt a cautious mood in psychologists too; for, philosophically considered, what do we mean by the "limitedness of space" if not a relativization of the space category? Something similar might easily happen to the category of time (and to that of causality as well).[2] Doubts about these matters are more warranted today than ever before.

815   The nature of the psyche reaches into obscurities far beyond the scope of our understanding. It contains as many riddles as the universe with its galactic systems, before whose majestic configurations only a mind lacking in imagination can fail to admit its own insufficiency. This extreme uncertainty of human comprehension makes the intellectualistic hubbub not only ridiculous, but also deplorably dull. If, therefore, from the needs of his own heart, or in accordance with the ancient lessons of human wisdom, or out of respect for the psychological fact that "telepathic" perceptions occur, anyone should draw the conclusion that the psyche, in its deepest reaches, participates in a form of existence beyond space and time, and thus partakes of what is inadequately and symbolically described as "eternity" —then critical reason could counter with no other argument than the "non liquet" of science. Furthermore, he would have the inestimable advantage of conforming to a bias of the human psyche which has existed from time immemorial and is universal. Anyone who does not draw this conclusion, whether

[2] [Cf. "Synchronicity: An Acausal Connecting Principle," pars. 816ff., in C.W. 8.—Editors.]

from scepticism or rebellion against tradition, from lack of courage or inadequate psychological experience or thoughtless ignorance, stands very little chance, statistically, of becoming a pioneer of the mind, but has instead the indubitable certainty of coming into conflict with the truths of his blood. Now whether these are in the last resort absolute truths or not we shall never be able to determine. It suffices that they are present in us as a "bias," and we know to our cost what it means to come into unthinking conflict with these truths. It means the same thing as the conscious denial of the instincts—uprootedness, disorientation, meaninglessness, and whatever else these symptoms of inferiority may be called. One of the most fatal of the sociological and psychological errors in which our time is so fruitful is the supposition that something can become entirely different all in a moment; for instance, that man can radically change his nature, or that some formula or truth might be found which would represent an entirely new beginning. Any essential change, or even a slight improvement, has always been a miracle. Deviation from the truths of the blood begets neurotic restlessness, and we have had about enough of that these days. Restlessness begets meaninglessness, and the lack of meaning in life is a soul-sickness whose full extent and full import our age has not as yet begun to comprehend.

PSYCHOLOGY AND SPIRITUALISM[1]

⁷⁴⁶ The reader should not casually lay this book aside on discovering that it is about "Invisibles," that is to say about spirits, on the assumption that it belongs to the literature of spiritualism. One can very well read the book without resorting to any such hypothesis or theory, and take it simply as a report of psychological facts or a continuous series of communications from the unconscious—which is, indeed, what it is really about. Even spirits appear to be psychic phenomena whose origins lie in the unconscious. At all events, the "Invisibles" who are the source of information in this book are shadowy personifications of unconscious contents, conforming to the rule that activated portions of the unconscious assume the character of *personalities* when they are perceived by the conscious mind. For this reason, the voices heard by the insane seem to belong to definite personalities who can often be identified, and personal intentions are attributed to them. And in fact, if the observer is able—though this is not always easy—to collect together a fair number of these verbal hallucinations, he will discover in them something very like motives and intentions of a personal character.

⁷⁴⁷ The same is true to an even greater degree of the "controls" in mediumistic séances who make the "communications." Everything in our psyche has to begin with a personal character, and one must push one's investigations very far before one comes across elements that are no longer personal. The "I" or "we" of these communications has a merely grammatical significance and is never proof of the existence of a spirit, but only of the physical presence

[1] [First published as the foreword to Stewart Edward White, *Uneingeschränktes Weltall* (Zurich, 1948), the German trans. of *The Unobstructed Universe* (New York, 1940), in which a foreword by Jung had not appeared. It was subsequently published as "Psychologie und Spiritismus," *Neue Schweizer Rundschau*, n.s., XVI:7 (Nov., 1948), 430–35. White (1873–1946), American author, chiefly wrote adventure stories with a frontier background; he became involved with spiritualism later in life. Jung was introduced to his books in 1946 by Fritz Künkel, American psychotherapist; see his letter to Künkel, 10 July 1946, discussing *The Unobstructed Universe* at length, in *C. G. Jung: Letters*, ed. G. Adler, vol. I.]

of the medium or mediums. In dealing with "proofs of identity," such as are offered in this book, one must remember that proofs of this kind would seem to be theoretically impossible considering the enormous number of possible sources of error. We know for a certainty that the unconscious is capable of subliminal perceptions and is a treasure house of lost memories. In addition, it has been proved by experiment that time and space are *relative* for the unconscious, so that unconscious perception, not being impeded by the space-time barrier, can obtain experiences to which the conscious mind has no access. In this connection I would refer to the experiments conducted at Duke University and other places.[2]

748   Considering all this, the proof of identity seems to be a forlorn hope, in theory anyway. In practice, however, things are rather different because cases actually occur which are so overwhelmingly impressive that they are absolutely convincing to those concerned. Even though our critical arguments may cast doubt on every single case, there is not a single argument that could prove that spirits do not exist. In this regard, therefore, we must rest content with a "non liquet." Those who are convinced of the reality of spirits should know that this is a subjective opinion which can be attacked on any number of grounds. Those who are not convinced should beware of naïvely assuming that the whole question of spirits and ghosts has been settled and that all manifestations of this kind are meaningless swindles. This is not so at all. These phenomena exist in their own right, regardless of the way they are interpreted, and it is beyond all doubt that they are genuine manifestations of the unconscious. The communications of "spirits" are *statements about the unconscious psyche,* provided that they are really spontaneous and are not cooked up by the conscious mind. They have this in common with dreams; for dreams, too, are statements about the unconscious, which is why the psychotherapist uses them as a first-class source of information.

749   *The Unobstructed Universe* may therefore be regarded as offering valuable information about the unconscious and its ways. It differs very favourably from the usual run of spiritualistic communications in that it eschews all edifying verbiage and concentrates instead on certain general ideas. This pleasing difference may be attributable to the happy circumstance that the real begetter of the book is the medium Betty, the deceased wife of the author.

[2] J. B. Rhine, *New Frontiers of the Mind* (1937); *The Reach of the Mind* (1948). Also G.N.M. Tyrrell, *The Personality of Man* (1947).

It is her "spirit" that pervades the book. We are familiar with her personality from Mr. White's earlier books,[3] and we know how great an educative influence she had on all those around her, constellating in their unconscious all the things that come to light in these communications.

750   The educative intention behind Betty's activity does not differ essentially from the general tenor of spiritualistic literature. The "spirits" strive to develop man's consciousness and to unite it with the unconscious, and Betty, on her own admission, pursues the same aim. It is interesting to note that the beginnings of American spiritualism coincided with the growth of scientific materialism in the middle of the nineteenth century. Spiritualism in all its forms therefore has a *compensatory* significance. Nor should it be forgotten that a number of highly competent scientists, doctors, and philosophers have vouched for the truth of certain phenomena which demonstrate the very peculiar effect the psyche has upon matter. Among them were Friedrich Zöllner, William Crookes, Alfred Richet, Camille Flammarion, Giovanni Schiaparelli, Sir Oliver Lodge, and our Zurich psychiatrist Eugen Bleuler, not to mention a large number of less well-known names. Although I have not distinguished myself by any original researches in this field, I do not hesitate to declare that I have observed a sufficient number of such phenomena to be completely convinced of their reality. To me they are inexplicable, and I am therefore unable to decide in favour of any of the usual interpretations.

751   Although I do not wish to prejudice the reader of this book, I cannot refrain from drawing attention to some of the issues it raises. What, above all, seems to me worth mentioning—especially in view of the fact that the author has no knowledge of modern psychology—is that the "Invisibles" favour an energic conception of the psyche which has much in common with recent psychological findings. The analogy is to be found in the idea of "frequency." But here we come upon a difference that should not be overlooked. For whereas the psychologist supposes that consciousness has a higher energy than the unconscious, the "Invisibles" attribute to the spirit of the departed (i.e., to a personified unconscious content) a higher "frequency" than to the living psyche. One should not, however, attach too much importance to the fact that the concept

---

[3] [*The Betty Book* (1937); *Across the Unknown* (1939); *The Road I Know* (1942).]

of energy is made use of in both cases, since this is a fundamental category of thought in all the modern sciences.

752   The "Invisibles" further assert that our world of consciousness and the "Beyond" together form a single cosmos, with the result that the dead are not in a different place from the living. There is only a difference in their "frequencies," which might be likened to the revolutions of a propeller: at low speeds the blades are visible, but at high speeds they disappear. In psychological terms this would mean that the conscious and the unconscious psyche are one, but are separated by different amounts of energy. Science can agree with this statement, although it cannot accept the claim that the unconscious possesses a higher energy since this is not borne out by experience.

753   According to the "Invisibles," the "Beyond" is this same cosmos but without the limitations imposed on mortal man by space and time. Hence it is called "the unobstructed universe." Our world is contained in this higher order and owes its existence principally to the fact that the corporeal man has a low "frequency," thanks to which the limiting factors of space and time become operative. The world without limitations is called "Orthos," which means the "right" or "true" world. This tells us clearly enough what kind of significance is imputed to the "Beyond," though it must be emphasized that this does not imply a devaluation of our world. I am reminded of the philosophical riddle which my Arab dragon-man asked me when visiting the tombs of the Khalifs in Cairo. "Which man is the cleverer: the one who builds his house where he will be for the longest time, or the one who builds it where he will be only temporarily?" Betty is in no doubt that this limited life should be lived as fully as possible, because the attainment of maximum consciousness while still in this world is an essential condition for the coming life in "Orthos." She is thus in agreement not only with the general trend of spiritualistic philosophy, but also with Plato, who regarded philosophy as a preparation for death.

754   Modern psychology can affirm that for many people this problem arises in the second half of life, when the unconscious often makes itself felt in a very insistent way. The unconscious is the land of dreams, and according to the primitive view the land of dreams is also the land of the dead and of the ancestors. From all we know about it, the unconscious does in fact seem to be relatively independent of space and time, nor is there anything objectionable in the idea that consciousness is surrounded by the sea

of the unconscious, just as this world is contained in "Orthos." The unconscious is of unknown extent and is possibly of greater importance than consciousness. At any rate, the role which consciousness plays in the life of primitives and primates is insignificant compared with that of the unconscious. The events in our modern world, as we see humanity blindly staggering from one catastrophe to the next, are not calculated to strengthen anyone's belief in the value of consciousness and the freedom of the will. Consciousness *should* of course be of supreme importance, for it is the only guarantee of freedom and alone makes it possible for us to avoid disaster. But this, it seems, must remain for the present a pious hope.

755   Betty's aim is to extend consciousness as far as possible by uniting it with "Orthos." To this end it must be trained to listen to the unconscious psyche in order to bring about the collaboration of the "Invisibles." The aims of modern psychotherapy are similar: it too endeavours to compensate the onesidedness and narrowness of the conscious mind by deepening its knowledge of the unconscious.

756   The similarity of aim should not, however, lead us to overlook a profound difference of viewpoint. The psychology of the "Betty Books" differs in no essential respect from the primitive view of the world, where the contents of the unconscious are all projected into external objects. What appears to the primitive to be a "spirit" may on a more conscious level be an abstract thought, just as the gods of antiquity turned into philosophical ideas at the beginning of our era. This primitive projection of psychological factors is common to both spiritualism and theosophy. The advantage of projection is obvious: the projected content is visibly "there" in the object and calls for no further reflection. But since the projection does bring the unconscious a bit nearer to consciousness, it is at least better than nothing. Mr. White's book certainly makes us think, but the kind of thinking it caters to is not psychological; it is mechanistic, and this is of little help when we are faced with the task of integrating projections. Mechanistic thinking is one of the many Americanisms that stamp the book as a typical product and leave one in no doubt as to its origin. But it is well worth while getting to know this side of the American psyche, for the world will hear a great deal more of it in times to come.

July 1948

FOREWORD TO MOSER:
"SPUK: IRRGLAUBE ODER WAHRGLAUBE?"[1]

⁷⁵⁷ The author has asked me for a few introductory words to her book. It gives me all the more pleasure to comply with her request as her previous book on occultism,[2] written with great care and knowledge of the subject, is still fresh in my memory. I welcome the appearance of this new book, a copiously documented collection of parapsychological experiences, as a valuable contribution to psychological literature in general. Extraordinary and mysterious stories are not necessarily always lies and fantasies. Many "ingenious, curious, and edifying tales" were known to previous centuries, among them observations whose scientific validity has since been confirmed. The modern psychological description of man as a totality had its precursors in the numerous biographical accounts of unusual people such as somnambulists and the like at the beginning of the nineteenth century. Indeed, though we owe the discovery of the unconscious to these old pre-scientific observations, our investigation of parapsychological phenomena is still in its infancy. We do not yet know the full range of the territory under discussion. Hence a collection of observations and of reliable material performs a very valuable service. The collector must certainly have courage and an unshakable purpose if he is not to be intimidated by the difficulties, handicaps, and possibilities of error that beset such an undertaking, and the reader, too, must summon up sufficient interest and patience to allow this sometimes disconcerting material to work upon him objectively, regardless of his prejudices. In this vast and shadowy region, where everything seems possible and nothing believable, one must oneself have observed many strange happenings and in addition heard, read, and if possible tested many stories by examining their witnesses in order to form an even moderately sure judgment.

⁷⁵⁸ In spite of such advances as the founding of the British and American Society for Psychical Research and the existence of a

---

[1] [Baden, 1950. By Fanny Moser. ("Ghost: False Belief or True?")]
[2] [*Okkultismus: Täuschungen und Tatsachen* (1935).]

considerable and in part well-documented literature, a prejudice is still rampant even in the best informed circles, and reports of this kind meet with a mistrust which is only partially justified. It looks as though Kant will be proved right for a long time to come when he wrote nearly two hundred years ago: "Stories of this kind will have at any time only secret believers, while publicly they are rejected by the prevalent fashion of disbelief."[3] He himself reserved judgment in the following words: "The same ignorance makes me so bold as to absolutely deny the truth of the various ghost stories, and yet with the common, although queer, reservation that while I doubt any one of them, still I have a certain faith in the whole of them taken together."[4] One could wish that very many of our bigots would take note of this wise position adopted by a great thinker.

759   I am afraid this will not come about so easily, for our rationalistic prejudice is grounded—*lucus a non lucendo*—not on reason but on something far deeper and more archaic, namely on a primitive instinct to which Goethe referred when he said in *Faust:* "Summon not the well-known throng . . ." I once had a valuable opportunity to observe this instinct at work. It was while I was with a tribe on Mount Elgon, in East Africa, most of whom had never come into contact with the white man. Once, during a palaver, I incautiously uttered the word *seleljteni,* which means "ghosts." Suddenly a deathly silence fell on the assembly. The men glanced away, looked in all directions, and some of them made off. My Somali headman and the chief confabulated together, and then the headman whispered in my ear: "What did you say that for? Now you'll have to break up the palaver." This taught me that one must never mention ghosts on any account. The same primitive fear of ghosts is still deep in our bones, but it is unconscious. Rationalism and superstition are complementary. It is a psychological rule that the brighter the light, the blacker the shadow; in other words, the more rationalistic we are in our conscious minds, the more alive becomes the spectral world of the unconscious. And it is indeed obvious that rationality is in large measure an apotropaic defence against superstition, which is everpresent and unavoidable. The daemonic world of primitives is only a few generations away from us, and the things that have happened and still go on happening in the dictator states teach us how terrifyingly close it is. I must constantly

[3] [*Dreams of a Spirit-Seer,* trans. by Goerwitz, p. 92.]
[4] [Ibid., p. 88.]

remind myself that the last witch was burned in Europe in the year my grandfather was born.

760   The widespread prejudice against the factual reports discussed in this book shows all the symptoms of the primitive fear of ghosts. Even educated people who should know better often advance the most nonsensical arguments, tie themselves in knots and deny the evidence of their own eyes. They will put their names to reports of séances and then—as has actually happened more than once— withdraw their signatures afterwards, because what they have witnessed and corroborated is nevertheless impossible—as though anyone knew exactly what is impossible and what is not!

761   Ghost stories and spiritualistic phenomena practically never prove what they seem to. They offer no proof of the immortality of the soul, which for obvious reasons is incapable of proof. But they are of interest to the psychologist from several points of view. They provide information about things the layman knows nothing of, such as the exteriorization of unconscious processes, about their content, and about the possible sources of parapsychological phenomena. They are of particular importance in investigating the localization of the unconscious and the phenomenon of synchronicity, which points to a relativation of space and time and hence also of matter. It is true that with the help of the statistical method existence of such effects can be proved, as Rhine and other investigators have done. But the individual nature of the more complex phenomena of this kind forbids the use of the statistical method, since this stands in a complementary relation to synchronicity and necessarily destroys the latter phenomenon, which the statistician is bound to discount as due to chance. We are thus entirely dependent on well observed and well authenticated individual cases. The psychologist can only bid a hearty welcome to any new crop of objective reports.

762   The author has put together an impressive collection of factual material in this book. It differs from other collections of the kind by its careful and detailed documentation, and thus gives the reader a total impression of the situation which he often looks for in vain in other reports of this nature. Although ghosts exhibit certain universal features they nevertheless appear in individual forms and under conditions which are infinitely varied and of especial importance for the investigator. The present collection provides the most valuable information in just this respect.

763   The question discussed here is a weighty one for the future.

Science has only just begun to take a serious interest in the human psyche and, more particularly, in the unconscious. The wide realm of psychic phenomena also includes parapsychology, which is opening undreamt-of vistas before our eyes. It is high time humanity took cognizance of the nature of the psyche, for it is becoming more and more evident that the greatest danger which threatens man comes from his own psyche and hence from that part of the empirical world we know the least about. Psychology needs a tremendous widening of its horizon. The present book is a milestone on the long road to knowledge of the psychic nature of man.

April 1950

Jung's Contribution[5]

764   In the summer of 1920 I went to London, at the invitation of Dr. X, to give some lectures. My colleague told me that, in expectation of my visit, he had found a suitable weekend place for the summer. This, he said, had not been so easy, because every thing had already been let for the summer holidays, or else was so exorbitantly expensive or unattractive that he had almost given up hope. But finally, by a lucky change, he had found a charming cottage that was just right for us, and at a ridiculously low price. In actual fact it turned out to be a most attractive old farmhouse in Buckinghamshire, as we saw when we went there at the end of our first week of work, on a Friday evening. Dr. X had engaged a girl from the neighbouring village to cook for us, and a friend of hers would come in the afternoons as a voluntary help. The house was roomy, two-storeyed, and built in the shape of a right angle. One of these wings was quite sufficient for us. On the ground floor there was a conservatory leading into the garden; then a kitchen, dining-room, and drawing-room. On the top floor a corridor ran from the conservatory steps through the middle of the house to a large bedroom, which took up the whole front of the wing. This was my room. It had windows facing east and west, and a fireplace in the front wall (north). To the left of the door stood a bed, opposite the fireplace a big old-fashioned chest of drawers, and to the right a wardrobe and a table. This, together with a few chairs, was all the furniture. On either side of the corridor

[5] [Pp. 253ff.]

was a row of bedrooms, which were used by Dr. X and occasional guests.

765   The first night, tired from the strenuous work of the week, I slept well. We spent the next day walking and talking. That evening, feeling rather tired, I went to bed at 11 o'clock, but did not get beyond the point of drowsing. I only fell into a kind of torpor, which was unpleasant because I felt I was unable to move. Also it seemed to me that the air had become stuffy, and that there was an indefinable, nasty smell in the room. I thought I had forgotten to open the windows. Finally, in spite of my torpor, I was driven to light a candle: both windows were open, and a night wind blew softly through the room, filling it with the flowery scents of high summer. There was no trace of the bad smell. I remained half awake in my peculiar condition, until I glimpsed the first pale light of dawn through the east window. At this moment the torpor dropped away from me like magic, and I fell into a deep sleep from which I awoke only towards nine o'clock.

766   On Sunday evening I mentioned in passing to Dr. X that I had slept remarkably badly the night before. He recommended me to drink a bottle of beer, which I did. But when I went to bed the same thing happened: I could not get beyond the point of drowsing. Both windows were open. The air was fresh to begin with, but after about half an hour it seemed to turn bad; it became stale and fuggy, and finally somehow repulsive. It was hard to identify the smell, despite my efforts to establish its nature. The only thing that came into my head was that there was something sickly about it. I pursued this clue through all the memories of smells that a man can collect in eight years of work at a psychiatric clinic. Suddenly I hit on the memory of an old woman who was suffering from an open carcinoma. This was quite unmistakably the same sickly smell I had so often noticed in her room.

767   As a psychologist, I wondered what might be the cause of this peculiar olfactory hallucination. But I was unable to discover any convincing connection between it and my present state of consciousness. I only felt very uncomfortable because my torpor seemed to paralyze me. In the end I could not think any more, and fell into a torpid doze. Suddenly I heard the noise of water dripping. "Didn't I turn off the tap properly?" I thought. "But of course, there's no running water in the room—so it's obviously raining—yet today was so fine." Meanwhile the dripping went on regularly, one drop every two seconds. I imagined a little pool of water to the

left of my bed, near the chest of drawers. "Then the roof must leak," I thought. Finally, with a heroic effort, so it seemed to me, I lit the candle and went over to the chest of drawers. There was no water on the floor, and no damp spot on the plaster ceiling. Only then did I look out of the window: it was a clear, starry night. The dripping still continued. I could make out a place on the floor, about eighteen inches from the chest of drawers, where the sound came from. I could have touched it with my hand. All at once the dripping stopped and did not come back. Towards three o'clock, at the first light of dawn, I fell into a deep sleep. No—I have heard death-watch beetles. The ticking noise they make is sharper. This was a duller sound, exactly what would be made by drops of water falling from the ceiling.

768   I was annoyed with myself, and not exactly refreshed by this weekend. But I said nothing to Dr. X. The next weekend, after a busy and eventful week, I did not think at all about my previous experience. Yet hardly had I been in bed for half an hour than everything was there as before: the torpor, the repulsive smell, the dripping. And this time there was something else: something brushed along the walls, the furniture creaked now here and now there, there were rustlings in the corners. A strange restlessness was in the air. I thought it was the wind, lit the candle and went to shut the windows. But the night was still, there was no breath of wind. So long as the light was on, the air was fresh and no noise could be heard. But the moment I blew out the candle, the torpor slowly returned, the air became fuggy, and the creakings and rustlings began again. I thought I must have noises in my ear, but at three o'clock in the morning they stopped as promptly as before.

769   The next evening I tried my luck again with a bottle of beer. I had always slept well in London and could not imagine what could give me insomnia in this quiet and peaceful spot. During the night the same phenomena were repeated, but in intensified form. The thought now occurred to me that they must be parapsychological. I knew that problems of which people are unconscious can give rise to exteriorization phenomena, because constellated unconscious contents often have a tendency to manifest themselves outwardly somehow or other. But I knew the problems of the present occupants of the house very well, and could discover nothing that would account for the exteriorizations. The next day I asked the others how they had slept. They all said they had slept wonderfully.

770   The third night it was even worse. There were loud knocking noises, and I had the impression that an animal, about the size of a dog, was rushing round the room in a panic. As usual, the hubbub stopped abruptly with the first streak of light in the east.

771   The phenomena grew still more intense during the following weekend. The rustling became a fearful racket, like the roaring of a storm. Sounds of knocking came also from outside in the form of dull blows, as though somebody were banging on the brick walls with a muffled hammer. Several times I had to assure myself that there was no storm, and that nobody was banging on the walls from outside.

772   The next weekend, the fourth, I cautiously suggested to my host that the house might be haunted, and that this would explain the surprisingly low rent. Naturally he laughed at me, although he was as much at a loss as I about my insomnia. It had also struck me how quickly the two girls cleared away after dinner every evening, and always left the house long before sundown. By eight o'clock there was no girl to be seen. I jokingly remarked to the girl who did the cooking that she must be afraid of us if she had herself fetched every evening by her friend and was then in such a hurry to get home. She laughed and said that she wasn't at all afraid of the gentlemen, but that nothing would induce her to stay a moment in this house alone, and certainly not after sunset. "What's the matter with it?" I asked. "Why, it's haunted, didn't you know? That's the reason why it was going so cheap. Nobody's ever stuck it here." It had been like that as long as she could remember. But I could get nothing out of her about the origin of the rumour. Her friend emphatically confirmed everything she had said.

773   As I was a guest, I naturally couldn't make further inquiries in the village. My host was sceptical, but he was willing to give the house a thorough looking over. We found nothing remarkable until we came to the attic. There, between the two wings of the house, we discovered a dividing wall, and in it a comparatively new door, about half an inch thick, with a heavy lock and two huge bolts, that shut off our wing from the unoccupied part. The girls did not know of the existence of this door. It presented something of a puzzle because the two wings communicated with one another both on the ground floor and on the first floor. There were no rooms in the attic to be shut off, and no signs of use. The purpose of the door seemed inexplicable.

774   The fifth weekend was so unbearable that I asked my host to

give me another room. This is what had happened: it was a beautiful moonlight night, with no wind; in the room there were rustlings, creakings, and bangings; from outside, blows rained on the walls. I had the feeling there was something near me, and opened my eyes. There, beside me on the pillow, I saw the head of an old woman, and the right eye, wide open, glared at me. The left half of the face was missing below the eye. The sight of it was so sudden and unexpected that I leapt out of bed with one bound, lit the candle, and spent the rest of the night in an armchair. The next day I moved into the adjoining room, where I slept splendidly and was no longer disturbed during this or the following weekend.

775   I told my host that I was convinced the house was haunted, but he dismissed this explanation with smiling scepticism. His attitude, understandable though it was, annoyed me somewhat, for I had to admit that my health had suffered under these experiences. I felt unnaturally fatigued, as I had never felt before. I therefore challenged Dr. X to try sleeping in the haunted room himself. He agreed to this, and gave me his word that he would send me an honest report of his observations. He would go to the house alone and spend the weekend there so as to give me a "fair chance."

776   Next morning I left. Ten days later I had a letter from Dr. X. He had spent the weekend alone in the cottage. In the evening it was very quiet, and he thought it was not absolutely necessary to go up to the first floor. The ghost, after all, could manifest itself anywhere in the house, if there was one. So he set up his camp bed in the conservatory, and as the cottage really was rather lonely, he took a loaded shotgun to bed with him. Everything was deathly still. He did not feel altogether at ease, but nevertheless almost succeeded in falling asleep after a time. Suddenly it seemed to him that he heard footsteps in the corridor. He immediately struck a light and flung open the door, but there was nothing to be seen. He went back grumpily to bed, thinking I had been a fool. But it was not long before he again heard footsteps, and to his discomfiture he discovered that the door lacked a key. He rammed a chair against the door, with its back under the lock, and returned to bed. Soon afterwards he again heard footsteps, which stopped just in front of the door; the chair creaked, as though somebody was pushing against the door from the other side. He then set up his bed in the garden, and there he slept very well. The next night he again put his bed in the garden, but at one o'clock it started to rain, so he shoved the head of the bed under the eaves of the conservatory

and covered the foot with a waterproof blanket. In this way he slept peacefully. But nothing in the world would induce him to sleep again in the conservatory. He had now given up the cottage.

777   A little later I heard from Dr. X that the owner had had the cottage pulled down, since it was unsaleable and scared away all tenants. Unfortunately I no longer have the original report, but its contents are stamped indelibly on my mind. It gave me considerable satisfaction after my colleague had laughed so loudly at my fear of ghosts.

*

778   I would like to make the following remarks by way of summing up. I can find no explanation of the dripping noise. I was fully awake and examined the floor carefully. I consider it out of the question that it was a delusion of the senses. As to the rustling and creaking, I think they were probably not objective noises, but noises in the ear which seemed to me to be occurring objectively in the room. In my peculiar hypnoid state they appeared exaggeratedly loud. I am not at all sure that the knocking noises, either, were objective. They could just as well have been heartbeats that seemed to me to come from outside. My torpor was associated with an inner excitation probably corresponding to fear. Of this fear I was unconscious until the moment of the vision—only then did it break through into consciousness. The vision had the character of a hypnagogic hallucination and was probably a reconstruction of the memory of the old woman with carcinoma.

779   Coming now to the olfactory hallucination, I had the impression that my presence in the room gradually activated something that was somehow connected with the walls. It seemed to me that the dog rushing round in a panic represented my intuition. Common speech links intuition with the nose: I had "smelt" something. If the olfactory organ in man were not so hopelessly degenerate, but as highly developed as a dog's, I would have undoubtedly have had a clearer idea of the persons who had lived in the room earlier. Primitive medicine-men can not only smell out a thief, they also "smell" spirits and ghosts.

780   The hypnoid catalepsy that each time was associated with these phenomena was the equivalent of intense concentration, the object of which was a subliminal and therefore "fascinating" olfactory perception. The two things together bear some resemblance to the

physical and psychic state of a pointer that has picked up the scent. The source of the fascination, however, seems to me to have been of a peculiar nature, which is not sufficiently explained by any substance emitting a smell. The smell may have "embodied" a psychic situation of an excitatory nature and carried it across to the percipient. This is by no means impossible when we consider the extraordinary importance of the sense of smell in animals. It is also conceivable that intuition in man has taken the place of the world of smells that were lost to him with the degeneration of the olfactory organ. The effect of intuition on man is indeed very similar to the instant fascination which smells have for animals. I myself have had a number of experiences in which "psychic smells," or olfactory hallucinations, turned out to be subliminal intuitions which I was able to verify afterwards.

781   This hypothesis naturally does not pretend to explain all ghost phenomena, but at most a certain category of them. I have heard and read a great many ghost stories, and among them are a few that could very well be explained in this way. For instance, there are all those stories of ghosts haunting rooms where a murder was committed. In one case, bloodstains were still visible under the carpet. A dog would surely have smelt the blood and perhaps recognized it as human, and if he possessed a human imagination he would also have been able to reconstruct the essential features of the crime. Our unconscious, which possesses very much more subtle powers of perception and reconstruction than our conscious minds, could do the same thing and project a visionary picture of the psychic situation that excited it. For example, a relative once told me that, when stopping at a hotel on a journey abroad, he had a fearful nightmare of a woman being murdered in his room. The next morning he discovered that on the night before his arrival a woman had in fact been murdered there. These remarks are only meant to show that parapsychology would do well to take account of the modern psychology of the unconscious.

FOREWORD TO JAFFÉ:
"APPARITIONS AND PRECOGNITION"[1]

782   The author of this book has already made a name for herself by her valuable contributions to the literature of analytical psychology. Here she tells of strange tales which incur the odium of superstition and are therefore exchanged only in secret. They were lured into the light of day by a questionnaire sent out by the *Schweizerischer Beobachter,* which can thereby claim to have rendered no small service to the public. The mass of material that came in arrived first at my address. Since my age and my evergrowing preoccupation with other matters did not allow me to burden myself with further work, the task of sorting out such a collection and submitting it to psychological evaluation could not have been placed in worthier hands than those of the author. She had displayed so much psychological tact, understanding and insight in her approach to a related theme—an interpretation of E.T.A. Hoffmann's story "The Golden Pot"[2]—that I never hesitated in my choice.

783   Curiously enough, the problem of wonder tales as they are currently told—enlightenment or no enlightenment—has never been approached from the psychological side. I naturally don't count mythology, although people are generally of the opinion that mythology is essentially history and no longer happens nowadays. As a psychic phenomenon of the present, it is considered merely a hunting-ground for economics. Nevertheless, ghost stories, warning visions, and other strange happenings are constantly being reported, and the number of people to whom something once "happened" is surprisingly large. Moreover, despite the disapproving silence of the "enlightened," it has not remained hidden from the wider public that for some time now there has been a serious science which goes by the name of "parapsychology." This fact may have helped to encourage the popular response to the questionnaire.

[1] [Aniela Jaffé, *Geistererscheinungen und Vorzeichen* (Zurich, 1958). Trans., New Hyde Park, New York, 1963, with the present trans. of the foreword, here somewhat revised.]

[2] "Bilder und Symbole aus E.T.A. Hoffmanns Märchen 'Der goldne Topf,'" in Jung, *Gestaltungen des Unbewussten* (1950).

784   One of the most notable things that came to light is the fact that among the Swiss, who are commonly regarded as stolid, unimaginative, rationalistic and materialistic, there are just as many ghost stories and suchlike as, say, in England or Ireland. Indeed, as I know from my own experience and that of other investigators, magic as practised in the Middle Ages and harking back to much remoter times has by no means died out, but still flourishes today as rampantly as it did centuries ago. One doesn't speak of these things, however, They simply happen, and the intellectuals know nothing of them—for intellectuals know neither themselves nor people as they really are. In the world of the latter, without their being conscious of it, the life of the centuries lives on, and things are continually happening that have accompanied human life from time immemorial: premonitions, foreknowledge, second sight, hauntings, ghosts, return of the dead, bewitchings, sorcery, magic spells, etc.

785   Naturally enough our scientific age wants to know whether such things are "true," without taking into account what the nature of any such proof would have to be and how it could be furnished. For this purpose the events in question must be looked at squarely and soberly, and it generally turns out that the most exciting stories vanish into thin air and what is left over is "not worth talking about." Nobody thinks of asking the fundamental question: what is the real reason why the same old stories are experienced and repeated over and over again, without losing any of their prestige? On the contrary, they return with their youthful vitality constantly renewed, fresh as on the first day.

786   The author has made it her task to take these tales for what they are, that is, as *psychic facts,* and not to pooh-pooh them because they do not fit into our scheme of things. She has therefore logically left aside the question of truth, as has long since been done in mythology, and instead has tried to inquire into the psychological questions: Exactly *who* is it that sees a ghost? Under what psychic conditions does he see it? What does a ghost signify when examined for its content, i.e., as a symbol?

787   She understands the art of leaving the story just as it is, with all the trimmings that are so offensive to the rationalist. In this way the *twilight atmosphere* that is so essential to the story is preserved. An integral component of any nocturnal, numinous experience is the dimming of consciousness, the feeling that one is in the grip of something greater than oneself, the impossibility of exercising

criticism, and the paralysis of the will. Under the impact of the experience reason evaporates and another power spontaneously takes control—a most singular feeling which one willy-nilly hoards up as a secret treasure no matter how much one's reason may protest. That, indeed, is the uncomprehended purpose of the experience—to make us feel the overpowering presence of a mystery.

788 The author has succeeded in preserving the total character of such experiences, despite the refractory nature of the reports, and in making it an object of investigation. Anyone who expects an answer to the question of parapsychological truth will be disappointed. The psychologist is little concerned here with what kind of facts can be established in the conventional sense; all that matters to him is whether a person will vouch for the authenticity of his experience regardless of all interpretations. The reports leave no doubt about this; moreover, in most cases their authenticity is confirmed by independent parallel stories. It cannot be doubted that such reports are found at all times and places. Hence there is no sufficient reason for doubting the veracity of individual reports. Doubt is justified only when it is a question of a deliberate lie. The number of such cases is increasingly small, for the authors of such falsifications are too ignorant to be able to lie properly.

789 The psychology of the unconscious has thrown so many beams of light into other dark corners that we would expect it to elucidate also the obscure world of wonder tales eternally young. From the copious material assembled in this book those conversant with depth psychology will surely gain new and significant insights which merit the greatest attention. I can recommend it to all those who know how to value things that break through the monotony of daily life with salutary effects, (sometimes!) shaking our certitudes and lending wings to the imagination.

August 1957

THE FUTURE OF PARAPSYCHOLOGY

The *International Journal of Parapsychology* (New York), in its 1963 autumn issue (V:4, pp. 450f.), published Jung's answers to a questionnaire which had been circulated in June 1960 among various authorities in connection with a survey on "The Future of Parapsychology."

How do you define parapsychology?

1213   Parapsychology is the science dealing with those biological or psychological events which show that the categories of matter, space, and time (and thus of causality) are not axiomatic.

Which areas of research, in your opinion, should be classified as belonging within parapsychology?

1214   The psychology of the unconscious.

Do you anticipate that future research would emphasize quantitative or qualitative work?

1215   Future research will have to emphasize both.

Do you believe that a repeatable *experiment is essential to strengthen the position of parapsychological studies within the scientific community?*

1216   The repeatable experiment is desirable but, inasmuch as most of the events are spontaneous and irregular, the experimental method will not be generally applicable.

Have you any comments on recent criticisms with regard to statistical methods employed in parapsychological studies?

1217   The statistical method is most desirable and indispensable to scientific research, where and when it can be applied. But this is only possible when the material shows a certain regularity and comparability.

Do you believe that certain qualitative researches may be quantified in order to gain wider acceptance?

1218   The quantification of qualitative research is surely the best means of conviction.

In the qualitative area, where do you foresee the greatest potential for future research progress—spontaneous phenomena, crisis telepathy, survival studies, out-of-the-body experiences, or any other?

219 The greatest and most important part of parapsychological research will be the careful exploration and qualitative description of spontaneous events.

Do you feel that during the past decade parapsychology has become more widely accepted among scientists active in other areas?

220 My impression is that, in Europe, at least, open-mindedness has increased.

Have you any comments regarding the psychological significance of certain psychic phenomena?

221 The psychological significance of parapsychological events has hardly been explored yet.

Have you any comments regarding the special psychological conditions that seem to favour, or reduce, the likelihood of an occurrence of psychic phenomena?

222 The factor which favours the occurrence of parapsychological events is the presence of an active archetype, i.e., a situation in which the deeper, instinctual layers of the psyche are called into action. The archetype is a borderline phenomenon, characterized by a relativation of space and time, as already pointed out by Albertus Magnus (*De mirabilibus mundi*),[1] whom I have mentioned in my paper "Synchronicity: An Acausal Connecting Principle."

[1] [Incunabulum, undated, Zentralbibliothek, Zurich. Cf. C.W., vol. 8, par. 859.]

BIBLIOGRAPHY

The items of the bibliography are arranged alphabetically under two headings: *A*. List of periodicals cited, with abbreviations; *B*. General bibliography, including both books and articles. It has not been possible to establish the full names of some medical writers cited in the early literature.

A. LIST OF PERIODICALS CITED, WITH ABBREVIATIONS

Allg Z f Psych = Allgemeine Zeitschrift für Psychiatrie und psychisch-gerichtliche Medicin. Berlin.

Ann méd-psych = Annales médico-psychologiques. Paris.

Arch f Psych und Nerv = Archiv für Psychiatrie und Nervenkrankheiten. Berlin.

Arch de neur = Archives de neurologie. Paris.

Jahrb f Psych = Jahrbuch für Psychiatrie und Neurologie. Leipzig and Vienna.

Journ f Psych u Neur = Journal für Psychologie und Neurologie. Leipzig. (A continuation of the *Zeitschrift für Hypnotismus*, q.v.)

Münch med Wochenschr = Münchener Medicinische Wochenschrift. Munich.

Neur Centralbl = Neurologisches Centralblatt. Berlin.

Proc Soc Psych Res = Proceedings of the Society for Psychical Research. London.

Prog méd = Progrès médical. Paris.

Rev de l'hyp = Revue de l'hypnotisme. Paris.

Rev phil = Revue philosophique de France et de l'Étranger. Paris.

Trans Coll Phys Philadelphia = Transactions of the College of Physicians of Philadelphia.

Trib méd = Tribune médicale. Paris.

Union méd = Union médicale. Paris.

Wiener med Presse = *Wiener medizinische Presse.* Vienna.

Z f Hyp = *Zeitschrift für Hypnotismus, Psychotherapie, etc.* Leipzig. (Continued as the *Journal für Psychologie und Neurologie,* q.v.)

B. GENERAL BIBLIOGRAPHY

AKSAKOW, ALEX. N. *Animismus und Spiritismus.* Leipzig, 1894.

AMMIANUS MARCELLINUS. *History.* Translated by John C. Rolfe (Loeb Classical Library) Cambridge (Mass.) and London, 1956.

ANONYMOUS. *Die Tyroler ekstatischen Jungfrauen. Leitsterne in die dunklen Gebiete der Mystik.* Regensburg, 1843.

AZAM, C. M. ÉTIENNE EUGÈNE. *Hypnotisme, double conscience, et altérations de la personnalité.* Paris, 1887.

BAETZ, E. VON. "Über Emotionslähmung," *Allg Z f Psych,* LVIII (1901), 177ff.

BAIN, ALEXANDER. *The Senses and the Intellect.* London, 1855.

BALLET, GILBERT. *Le Langage intérieur et les formes diverses de l'aphasie.* Paris, 1886.

―――. *Swedenborg. Histoire d'un visionaire au XVIII siècle.* Paris, 1899.

BEHR, ALBERT. "Bemerkungen über Erinnerungsfälschungen und pathologische Traumzustände," *Allg Z f Psych,* LVI (1899), 918ff.

BINET, ALFRED. *Alterations of Personality.* Translated by Helen Green Baldwin. London, 1896. (Original: *Les Altérations de la personnalité.* Paris, 1892.)

BOETEAU, M. "Automatisme somnambulique avec dédoublement de la personnalité," *Ann méd-psych,* 7th ser., V, 50th year (1892), 63–79.

BOHN, WOLFGANG. *Ein Fall von doppeltem Bewusstsein.* Dissertation, Breslau, 1898.

BONAMAISON, L. "Un Cas remarquable d'hypnose spontanée, etc.," *Rev de l'hyp,* 4th year (Feb., 1890), 234–43.

BOURRU, HENRI, and BUROT, FERDINAND. *Variations de la personnalité.* Paris, 1888.

BRESLER, JOHANN. "Kulturhistorischer Beitrag zur Hysterie," *Allg Z f Psych,* LIII (1896), 333ff.

BREUER, JOSEF, and FREUD, SIGMUND. *Studies on Hysteria.* Translated under the editorship of James Strachey. (Standard Edition of the Complete Psychological Works of Sigmund Freud, 2.) London and New York, 1955. (Original: *Studien über Hysterie.* Leipzig and Vienna, 1895.)

CAPRON, ELIAB WILKINSON. *Modern Spiritualism; its Facts and Fanaticisms, its Consistencies and Contradictions.* New York and Boston, 1855.

CARDAN, JEROME (Girolamo Cardano *or* Hieronymus Cardanus). *De subtilitate libri III.* Nuremberg, 1550. (Other editions: Paris, 1550, 1551; Basel, 1554, 1560, 1582, 1611; Lyons, 1580.)

CASSINI, JACQUES DOMINIQUE, COMTE DE THURY. *Les Tables parlantes au point de vue de la physique générale.* Paris, 1855.

[CELLINI, BENVENUTO.] *The Life of Benvenuto Cellini, Written by Himself.* Translated by John Addington Symonds. London (Phaidon Press), 1949.

CROOKES, WILLIAM. "Notes of an Enquiry into the Phenomena called Spiritual, during the years 1870–73," *Quarterly Journal of Science.* London, XI (n.s., IV) (1874).

CULLERRE, A. "Un Cas de somnambulisme hystérique," *Ann méd-psych,* 7th ser., VII, 46th year (1888), 354–70. (Reviewed by H. Kurella in *Allg Z f Psych,* XLVI (1890), p. 356* [Litteraturbericht].)

DELBRÜCK, ANTON. *Die pathologische Lüge und die psychisch abnormen Schwindler.* Stuttgart, 1891.

DESSOIR, MAX. *Das Doppel-Ich.* Berlin, 1890. (2nd edition, Berlin, 1896.)

DIEHL, AUGUST. "Neurasthenische Krisen," *Münch med Wochenschr,* 49th year, no. 9 (March, 1902), 363–66.

DONATH, JULIUS. "Über Suggestibilität," *Wiener med Presse,* 1892, no. 31, cols. 1244–46. (Cited in the next work.)

ECKERMANN, J. P. *Conversations with Goethe.* Translated by R. O. Moon. London, n.d. [1951].

EMMINGHAUS, H. *Allgemeine Psychopathologie zur Einführung in das Studium der Geistesstörungen.* Leipzig, 1878.

ERLER, ——. "Hysterisches und hystero-epileptisches Irresein," *Allg Z f Psych,* XXXV (1879), 16–45.

FLAUBERT, GUSTAVE. *Salammbô.* Translated by J. S. Chartres. London (Everyman's Library), 1931. (Original: Paris, 1862.)

FLOURNOY, THÉODORE. *From India to the Planet Mars.* Translated by D. B. Vermilye. New York and London, 1900. (Original: *Des Indes à la Planète Mars. Étude sur un cas de somnambulisme avec glossolalie.* Paris and Geneva, 1900.)

FOREL, AUGUSTE. *Hypnotism, or Suggestion and Psychotherapy.* Translated from the 5th German edition by H. W. Armit. London and New York, 1906. (Original: *Der Hypnotismus, seine . . . Bedeutung und . . . Handhabung.* Stuttgart, 1889. Later editions, 1891, 1911, 1918, etc.)

FREUD, SIGMUND. *The Interpretation of Dreams.* Translated by James Strachey. (Standard Edition, 4 and 5.) London and New York, 1953. 2 vols. (Original: *Die Traumdeutung.* Leipzig and Vienna, 1900.)

————. *The Freud/Jung Letters.* Edited by William McGuire. Translated by Ralph Manheim and R.F.C. Hull. Princeton (Bollingen Series XCIV) and London, 1974.

————. See also BREUER.

GOETHE, J. W. VON. *Elective Affinities.* A translation of *Die Wahlverwandtschaften.* With an introduction by Victoria C. Woodhull. Boston, 1872.

————. *Zur Naturwissenschaft. Allgemeine Naturlehre.* Stuttgart and Tübingen, 1817–23.

GÖRRES, JOHANN JOSEPH VON. *Die christliche Mystik.* Regensburg and Landshut, 1836–42. 4 vols.

————. *Emanuel Swedenborg, seine Visionen und sein Verhaltnis zur Kirch.* Speyer, 1827.

GRAETER, C. "Ein Fall von epileptischer Amnesie durch Hypermnesie beseitigt," *Z f Hyp, VIII* (1899), 129–63.

GUINON, GEORGES. "Documents pour servir à l'histoire des somnambulismes," *Prog méd,* 1891, XIII, 401–4, 425–29, 460–66, 513–17; XIV, 41–49, 137–41.

———— and WOLTKE, SOPHIE. "De l'influence des excitations des organes des sens sur les hallucinations de la phase passionnelle de l'attaque hystérique," *Arch de neur,* XXI: 63 (May, 1891), 346–65.

HAGEN, F. W. "Zur Theorie der Hallucination," *Allg Z f Psych,* XXV (1868), 1–113.

HAUPTMANN, CARL. *Die Bergschmiede.* Munich, 1902.

HECKER, JUSTUS FRIEDRICH CARL. *Über Visionen. Eine Vorlesung,* etc. Berlin, 1848.

HÖFELT, J. A. "Ein Fall von spontanem Somnambulismus," *Allg Z f Psych*, XLIX (1893), 250ff.

JAFFÉ, ANIELA. "Bilder und Symbole aus E. T. A. Hoffmanns Märchen 'Der goldne Topf,'" In: C. G. Jung, *Gestaltungen des Unbewussten*. Zurich, 1950.

JAMES, WILLIAM. *The Principles of Psychology*. New York and London, 1890. 2 vols.

JANET, PIERRE. "L'Anesthésie hystérique," *Arch de neur*, XXIII: 69 (May, 1892), 323–52.

———. *L'Automatisme psychologique*. 7th edition, Paris, 1913.

———. *The Mental State of Hystericals*. Translated by Caroline Rollin Corson. New York and London, 1901. (Original: *État mental des hystériques*. Paris, [1893].)

JESSEN, W. "Doppeltes Bewusstsein," *Allg Z f Psych*, XXII (1865), 407. (Report of address at Naturforscherversammlung zu Hannover, Psychiatrische Section, Sept. 18–23, 1865.)

JUNG, CARL GUSTAV. *Experimental Researches*. Coll. Works, 2.

———. *Gestaltungen des Unbewussten*. (With a contribution by Aniela Jaffé.) Zurich, 1950.

———. *Letters*. Selected and edited by Gerhard Adler, in collaboration with Aniela Jaffé. Translated by R.F.C. Hull. Princeton (Bollingen Series XCV) and London, 1973, 1975. 2 vols.

———. *Mysterium Coniunctionis*. Collected Works, 14.

———. "Studies in Word Association." Part I of *Experimental Researches*, q.v.

———. *Symbols of Transformation*. Collected Works, 5.

———. "Synchronicity: An Acausal Connecting Principle." In: *The Structure and Dynamics of the Psyche*. Coll. Works, 8.

———. *Two Essays on Analytical Psychology*. Collected Works, 7.

———. See also FREUD.

KANT, IMMANUEL. *Dreams of a Spirit-Seer, Illustrated by Dreams of Metaphysics*. Translated by Emanuel F. Goerwitz. New York and London, 1900.

[KANT, IMMANUEL.] *Kant's Cosmogony as in His "Essay on the Retardation of the Rotation of the Earth" and His "Natural History and Theory of the Heavens."* Edited and Translated by W. Hastie. Glasgow, 1900.

KARDEC, ALLAN. *Buch der Medien.* Translated by Emma A. Wood: *Experimental Spiritism. A Book on Mediums: Or, Guide for Mediums and Invocators.* Boston, 1874.

KARPLUS, J. P. "Über Pupillenstarre im hysterischen Anfalle," *Jahrb f Psych,* XVIII (1898), 1–53.

KERNER, JUSTINUS. *Blätter aus Prevorst.* Karlsruhe, 1831–39.

———. *Die Seherin von Prevorst.* Stuttgart and Tübingen, 1829. 2 vols. (Translation, not cited herein, by Mrs. [Catherine] Crowe: *The Seeress of Prevorst.* New York, 1859.)

———. *Die Geschichte des Thomas Ignaz Martin, Landsmanns zu Gallardon, über Frankreich und dessen Zukunft im Jahre 1816 geschaut.* Heilbronn, 1835.

———. *Die somnambulen Tische. Zur Geschichte und Erklärung dieser Erscheinungen.* Stuttgart, 1853.

KRAFFT-EBING, RICHARD VON. *Text-Book of Insanity based on Clinical Observations.* Authorized translation from the last German edition by C. G. Chaddock. Philadelphia, 1904. (Original: *Lehrbuch der Psychiatrie auf klinischer Grundlage,* Stuttgart, 1879. 7th edition, 1903.)

LADD, C. TRUMBULL. "Contribution to the Psychology of Visual Dreams," *Mind,* XVII (April, 1892), 299–304.

LEHMANN, ALFRED GEORG LUDWIG. *Aberglaube und Zauberei von den ältesten Zeiten an bis in die Gegenwart.* Translated from Danish by Dr. Petersen. Stuttgart, 1898.

LOEWENFELD, LEOPOLD. *Der Hypnotismus: Handbuch der Lehre von der Hypnose und der Suggestion.* Wiesbaden, 1901.

———. "Über hysterische Schlafzustände, deren Beziehungen zur Hypnose und zur Grande Hystérie," *Arch f Psych und Nerv,* XXII (1891), 715–38; XXIII (1892), 40–69.

MACARIO, M. M. A. "Des Hallucinations," *Ann méd-psych,* VI (1845), 317–49; VII (1846), 13–45. (Reviewed in *Allg Z f Psych,* IV [1848], 137ff.)

MACNISH, ROBERT. *The Philosophy of Sleep.* Glasgow, 1830.

MAURY, LOUIS FERDINAND ALFRED. *Le Sommeil et les rêves.* Paris, 1861. (3rd edition, Paris, 1865.)

MEIER, CARL ALFRED. "Spontanmanifestationen des kollektiven. Unbewussten," *Zentralblatt für Psychotherapie* (Leipzig), XI (1939), 284–303.

MESNET, ERNEST. "De l'automatisme de la mémoire et du souvenir dans la somnambulisme pathologique," *Union méd*, 3rd ser., XVIII: 87 (July 21, 1874), 105–112.

———. "Somnambulisme spontané dans ses rapports avec l'hystérie," *Arch de neur*, no. 69 (1892), 289–304.

MITCHELL, SILAS WEIR. "Mary Reynolds: A Case of Double Consciousness," *Trans Coll Phys Philadelphia*, 3rd ser., X (April 4, 1888), 366–89.

MOLL, ALBERT. "Die Bewusstseinsspaltung in Paul Lindau's neuem Schauspiel," *Z f Hyp*, I (1893), 306ff.

MÖRCHEN, FRIEDRICH. *Über Dämmerzustände*. Medical dissertation, Warburg, 1901.

MOSER, FANNY. *Der Okkultismus: Täuschungen und Tatsachen*. Munich, 1935.

MÜLLER, JOHANNES. *Über die phantastischen Gesichtserscheinungen*. Coblenz, 1826. (Cited in Hagen, "Zur Theorie der Hallucination," q.v.)

MYERS, FREDERIC W. H. "Automatic Writing," *Proc Soc Psych Res*, III (1885), 1–63.

NAEF, M. "Ein Fall von temporärer, totaler, theilweise retrograder Amnesie," *Z f Hyp*, VI (1897), 321–54.

NELKEN, JAN. "Analytische Beobachtungen über Phantasien eines Schizophrenen," *Jahrbuch für psychoanalytische und psychopathologische Forschungen* (Leipzig), IV (1912), 504–62.

NEUE PREUSSISCHE ZEITUNG.

NIETZSCHE, FRIEDRICH. *Thus Spake Zarathustra*. Translated by Thomas Common, revised by Oscar Levy and John L. Beevers. 6th edition, London, 1932. (Original: *Also Sprach Zarathustra*. 1883–91.)

———. *Ecce Homo*. Translated by A. M. Ludovici. London, 1927. (Original: 1888.)

PELMAN, C. "Über das Verhalten des Gedächtnisses bei den verschiedenen Formen des Irreseins," *Allg Z f Psych*, XXI (1864), 63–121.

PICK, ARNOLD. "Über pathologische Träumerei und ihre Beziehung zur Hysterie," *Jahrb f Psych*, XIV (1896), 280–330.

———. "Vom Bewusstsein in Zuständen sogenannter Bewusstlosigkeit," *Arch f Psych und Nerv*, XV (1884), 202–23.

PREYER, WILLIAM THIERRY. *Die Erklärung des Gedankenlesens*. Leipzig, 1886.

PRINCE, MORTON. "An Experimental Study of Visions," *Brain*, XXI (1898), 528ff.

PROUST, A. A. "Cas curieux d'automatisme ambulatoire chez un hystérique," *Trib méd*, 23rd year (March, 1890), 202–3.

QUICHERAT, JULES. *Procès de condamnation et de réhabilitation de Jeanne d'Arc, dite la Pucelle*, etc. Paris, 1841–49. 5 vols.

REDLICH, JOHANN. "Ein Beitrag zur Kenntnis der Pseudologia phantastica," *Allg Z f Psych*, LVI (1900), 65ff.

RHINE, J. B. *New Frontiers of the Mind*. New York, 1937. Reprinted Harmondsworth (Penguin Books), 1950.

———. *The Reach of the Mind*. New York and London, 1948. Reprinted Harmondsworth (Penguin Books), 1954.

RIBOT, THÉODULE ARMAND. *Die Persönlichkeit*. Translated from French by F. T. F. Pabst. Berlin, 1894.

RICHER, PAUL. *Études cliniques sur l'hystéro-epilepsie*. Paris, 1881.

RICHET, CHARLES. "La Suggestion mentale et le calcul des probabilités," *Rev phil*, XVIII (1884), II, 609–74.

RIEGER, CONRAD. *Der Hypnotismus*. Jena, 1884.

Samyutta-Nikaya. The Book of the Kindred Sayings. (Sangyutta-Nikaya). Translated by Mrs. C. A. F. Rhys Davids. London and New York, 1917–20.

SCHOPENHAUER, ARTHUR. *Parerga und Paralipomena*. Leipzig, 1874. Translated by E. F. J. Payne, Oxford, 1974.

———. *The World as Will and Idea*. Translated by R. B. Haldane and J. Kemp. (English and Foreign Philosophical Library, 22–24.) London, 1883–86. 3 vols. London, 6th edn., 1957. (Original: *Die Welt als Wille und Vorstellung*. (Sämtliche Werke, ed. by Eduard Grisebach, 6.)

SCHROEDER VAN DER KOLK, JACOBUS LUDOVICUS CONRADUS. *Die Pathologie und Therapie der Geisteskrankheiten auf anatomisch-physiologischer Grundlage*. Translated from Dutch by F. W. Theile. Brunswick, 1863. (Quoted in *Allg Z f Psych*, XXII [1865], 406–7.)

SCHÜLE, HEINRICH. *Handbuch der Geisteskrankheiten*. (Ziemssens Handbuch der speciellen Pathologie, etc., 16.) Leipzig, 1878.

SPIELREIN, S. "Über den psychischen Inhalt eines Falles von Schizophrenie," *Jahrbuch für psychoanalytische und psycho-*

pathologische Forschungen (Vienna and Leipzig), III (1911), 329–400.

STEFFENS, PAUL. "Über drei Fälle von 'Hysteria magna,'" *Arch f Psych und Nerv*, XXXIII (1900), 892–928.

TYRRELL, G. N. M. *The Personality of Man.* London, 1947.

WESTPHAL, A. "Über hysterische Dämmerzustände und das Symptom des 'Vorbeiredens,'" *Neur Centralbl*, XXI (1903), 7–16, 64–72.

WHITE, STEWART EDWARD. *Across the Unknown.* New York, 1939.

———. *The Betty Book.* New York, 1937. London, 1945.

———. *The Road I Know.* New York, 1942. London, 1951.

———. *The Unobstructed Universe.* New York, 1940. London, 1949.

WINSLOW, BENIGNUS FORBES. *Obscure Diseases of the Brain and Mind.* London, 1863. (Cited in *Allg Z f Psych*, XXII [1865], 405.)

ZSCHOKKE, JOHANN HEINRICH DANIEL. *Eine Selbstschau.* 3rd edition, Aarau, 1843.

ZÜNDEL, FRIEDRICH. *Pfarrer J. C. Blumhardt: Ein Lebensbild.* Zurich and Heilbronn, 1880.

THE COLLECTED WORKS OF

C. G. JUNG

T HE PUBLICATION of the first complete edition, in English, of the works of C. G. Jung was undertaken by Routledge and Kegan Paul, Ltd., in England and by Bollingen Foundation in the United States. The American edition is number XX in Bollingen Series, which since 1967 has been published by Princeton University Press. The edition contains revised versions of works previously published, such as *Psychology of the Unconscious*, which is now entitled *Symbols of Transformation*; works originally written in English, such as *Psychology and Religion*; works not previously translated, such as *Aion*; and, in general, new translations of virtually all of Professor Jung's writings. Prior to his death, in 1961, the author supervised the textual revision, which in some cases is extensive. Sir Herbert Read (d. 1968), Dr. Michael Fordham, and Dr. Gerhard Adler compose the Editorial Committee; the translator is R. F. C. Hull (except for Volume 2) and William McGuire is executive editor.

The price of the volumes varies according to size; they are sold separately, and may also be obtained on standing order. Several of the volumes are extensively illustrated. Each volume contains an index and in most a bibliography; the final volumes will contain a complete bibliography of Professor Jung's writings and a general index to the entire edition.

In the following list, dates of original publication are given in parentheses (of original composition, in brackets). Multiple dates indicate revisions.

* Published 1957; 2nd edn., 1970.   † Published 1973.

                                                             (continued)

* Published 1960.   † Published 1961.
‡ Published 1956; 2nd edn., 1967. (65 plates, 43 text figures.)

Psychological Factors Determining Human Behavior (1937)
Instinct and the Unconscious (1919)
The Structure of the Psyche (1927/1931)
On the Nature of the Psyche (1947/1954)
General Aspects of Dream Psychology (1916/1948)
On the Nature of Dreams (1945/1948)
The Psychological Foundations of Belief in Spirits (1920/1948)
Spirit and Life (1926)
Basic Postulates of Analytical Psychology (1931)
Analytical Psychology and *Weltanschauung* (1928/1931)
The Real and the Surreal (1933)
The Stages of Life (1930–1931)
The Soul and Death (1934)
Synchronicity: An Acausal Connecting Principle (1952)
Appendix: On Synchronicity (1951)

*9. PART I. THE ARCHETYPES AND THE
COLLECTIVE UNCONSCIOUS
Archetypes of the Collective Unconscious (1934/1954)
The Concept of the Collective Unconscious (1936)
Concerning the Archetypes, with Special Reference to the Anima
    Concept (1936/1954)
Psychological Aspects of the Mother Archetype (1938/1954)
Concerning Rebirth (1940/1950)
The Psychology of the Child Archetype (1940)
The Psychological Aspects of the Kore (1941)
The Phenomenology of the Spirit in Fairytales (1945/1948)
On the Psychology of the Trickster-Figure (1954)
Conscious, Unconscious, and Individuation (1939)
A Study in the Process of Individuation (1934/1950)
Concerning Mandala Symbolism (1950)
Appendix: Mandalas (1955)

*9. PART II. AION (1951)
RESEARCHES INTO THE PHENOMENOLOGY OF THE SELF
The Ego
The Shadow
The Syzygy: Anima and Animus
The Self
Christ, a Symbol of the Self
The Sign of the Fishes   *(continued)*

* Published 1959; 2nd edn., 1968. (Part I: 79 plates, with 29 in colour.)

* Published 1964; 2nd edn., 1970. (8 plates.)
† Published 1958; 2nd edn., 1969.

* Published 1953; 2nd edn., completely revised, 1968. (270 illustrations.)
† Published 1968. (50 plates, 4 text figures.)
‡ Published 1963; 2nd edn., 1970. (10 plates.)

* Published 1966.
† Published 1954; 2nd edn., revised and augmented, 1966. (13 illustrations.)
‡ Published 1954.

The Development of Personality (1934)
Marriage as a Psychological Relationship (1925)

*18. THE SYMBOLIC LIFE
Miscellaneous Writings

†19. GENERAL BIBLIOGRAPHY OF C. G. JUNG'S WRITINGS

†20. GENERAL INDEX TO THE COLLECTED WORKS

See also:

C. G. JUNG: LETTERS
Selected and edited by Gerhard Adler, in collaboration with Aniela Jaffé.
Translations from the German by R.F.C. Hull.

VOL. 1: 1906–1950
VOL. 2: 1951–1961

THE FREUD/JUNG LETTERS
Edited by William McGuire, translated by
Ralph Manheim and R.F.C. Hull

C. G. JUNG SPEAKING: Interviews and Encounters
Edited by William McGuire and R.F.C. Hull

C. G. JUNG: Word and Image
Edited by Aniela Jaffé

* Published 1976.
† Published 1979.